Improving Vocabulary Skills

Short Version

Fifth Edition

Improving Vocabulary Skills

Short Version

Fifth Edition

Eliza Comodromos
Paul Langan

Additional Materials from Townsend Press

PRINT

Reading Skills

Groundwork for College Reading with Phonics
Groundwork for College Reading
Ten Steps to Building College Reading Skills
Ten Steps to Improving College Reading Skills
Ten Steps to Advancing College Reading Skills
Ten Steps to Mastering College Reading Skills

Vocabulary Skills

Vocabulary Basics
Groundwork for a Better Vocabulary
Building Vocabulary Skills
Building Vocabulary Skills, Short Version
Improving Vocabulary Skills
Improving Vocabulary Skills, Short Version
Advancing Vocabulary Skills
Advancing Vocabulary Skills, Short Version
Advanced Word Power

English, Grammar, and Writing Skills

English Essentials
The Reading-Writing Connection
The Advanced Reading-Writing Connection
Voices and Values: A Reader for Writers

Print Supplement (for Most Books)

Instructor's Edition

DIGITAL

Reading Skills

Ten Steps Plus
Ten Steps Plus LE, Limited Edition
College Reading Essentials Plus

Vocabulary Skills

Vocabulary Plus

English, Grammar, and Writing Skills

English Essentials Plus
Reading-Writing Plus
Reading-Writing Plus LE, Limited Edition

Digital Assessments

College Reading Test (4 forms)
Basic Written English Test (2 forms)
Vocabulary Placement Test

Digital Supplements (for Most Books)

Instructor's Manual and Test Bank
PowerPoints
eBooks

Copyright © 2018 by Townsend Press, Inc.
Printed in the United States of America
9 8 7 6 5 4 3 2 1

ISBN-13 (Student Edition): 978-1-59194-537-6
ISBN-13 (Instructor's Edition): 978-1-59194-538-3

Send book orders and requests for desk copies or supplements to:

Townsend Press Book Center
439 Kelley Drive
West Berlin, New Jersey 08091

For even faster service, contact us in any of the following ways:

By telephone: 1-800-772-6410
By fax: 1-800-225-8894
By email: cs@townsendpress.com
Through our website: www.townsendpress.com

Contents

NOTE: Each of the chapters presents ten words apiece. For ease of reference, the title of the selection that closes each chapter is included.

Unit Four

Appendixes

Preface: To the Instructor

Words have power. They express our emotions, convey our ideas, articulate our opinions, and reveal our thoughts. Students without an expansive vocabulary are challenged when asked to do these tasks. Furthermore, weak vocabularies limit students' understanding of what they read and the clarity of what they write. Many teachers tell us that their students' vocabularies are inadequate for academic demands.

Improving Vocabulary Skills, Short Version aims to correct this problem. Spanning 20 chapters divided into 4 units, it teaches 200 important words. Here are the book's distinctive features:

1 **An intensive words-in-context approach.** Studies show that students learn words best by reading them repeatedly in different contexts, not through rote memorization. The book gives students an intensive in-context experience by presenting each word in *at least* **six** different contexts. Each chapter takes students through a productive sequence of steps:

- Students infer the meaning of each word by considering two sentences in which it appears and then choosing from multiple-choice options.
- On the basis of their inferences, students identify each word's meaning in a matching test. They are then in a solid position to deepen their knowledge of a word.
- Finally, they strengthen their understanding of a word by using it three times: in two sentence-length practices and in one longer passage. Each encounter with a word brings it closer to becoming part of the student's permanent word bank.

2 **Abundant practice.** Along with extensive practice in each chapter, there are a crossword puzzle and a set of unit tests at the end of every five-chapter unit. The puzzle and tests reinforce students' knowledge of the words in each unit. In addition, subsequent chapters revisit words from earlier chapters (repeated words are marked with small circles, like this°), allowing for more reinforcement. Last, there are supplementary tests in the *Instructor's Manual and Test Bank,* which is available in the Learning Center to instructors as a downloadable PDF. All this practice means that students learn in the surest possible way: by working closely and repeatedly with each word. And if you prefer even more practice, *Vocabulary Plus*—our digital word-building program—is available. See page viii for details.

3 **Controlled feedback and opportunities for independent learning.** The opening activity in each chapter gives students three multiple-choice options to help them decide on the meaning of a given word. This activity also helps students complete the matching exercise that is the second activity of each chapter. A limited answer key at the back of the book then provides answers for the third activity in the chapter. All these features enable students to take an active role in their own learning.

4 **Focus on essential words.** A good deal of time and research went into selecting the words and word parts in each book in the Vocabulary Series. Word frequency lists were consulted, along with word banks in a wide range of vocabulary books. In addition, the authors and editors each prepared their own lists based on their teaching experience. A lengthy process of data consolidation followed by group discussion then led to final decisions about the words and word parts that would be most helpful for students on each level.

5 **Appealing content.** Dull practice materials work against learning. On the other hand, meaningful, lively, and at times even funny sentences and passages can spark students' attention and enhance their grasp of the material. For this reason, a great deal of effort was put into creating sentences and passages with both widespread appeal and solid context support. We have tried throughout to make the practice materials truly enjoyable for teachers and students alike.

6 **Clear format.** The book has been designed so that its very format contributes to the learning process. Each chapter consists of two two-page spreads. In the first spread (see pages 8–9), students can easily refer to all ten words in context while working on the matching activity, which provides a clear meaning for each word. In the second spread (see pages 10–11), students can refer to a box that shows all ten words while they work through the fill-in activities on these pages.

7 **Supplementary materials.**

   a A convenient *Instructor's Edition* is available at no charge to educators using the book. It is identical to the student book except that it contains answers to all of the activities and tests.

   b A downloadable electronic (PDF) *Instructor's Manual and Test Bank* is also offered to instructors at no charge in the Learning Center (www.townsendpress.net). This digital supplement contains a general vocabulary placement test, along with a pretest and a posttest for the entire book as well as for each of its five units. It also includes teaching guidelines, suggested syllabi, an answer key, and an additional mastery test for each chapter and for each unit.

   c *PowerPoint presentations* are available for this book and may be downloaded at no charge from the Learning Center. Educators must have an approved instructor account to access this material. The PowerPoints can be used in class to give students a visual introduction to the words and word parts of each chapter in their text.

   d *eBooks* of student editions of all titles in the Vocabulary Series are available in the Learning Center as a free reference copy of the class text whenever educators need it. To learn more about the various digital supplements and other products, visit www.townsendpress.com or contact Customer Service (see below).

8 **Realistic pricing.** As with the previous editions, the goal has been to offer the highest possible quality at the lowest possible price. While *Improving Vocabulary Skills* is comprehensive enough to serve as a primary text, its modest price also makes it an inexpensive supplement.

9 **One in a sequence of books.** The most fundamental book in the Townsend Press vocabulary series is *Vocabulary Basics*. It is followed by *Groundwork for a Better Vocabulary* (a slightly more advanced basic text) and then by the three main books in the series: *Building Vocabulary Skills* (also a basic text), *Improving Vocabulary Skills* (an intermediate text), and *Advancing Vocabulary Skills* (a more advanced text). The most advanced book in the Townsend Press vocabulary series is *Advanced Word Power*. There are also short versions of the *Building, Improving*, and *Advancing* books. Suggested grade levels for the books can be found on our website or in the *Instructor's Manual*. Together, the books can help create a vocabulary foundation that will make any student a better reader, writer, and thinker.

10 **Digital options.** Looking for a paperless way to teach vocabulary? We've got it. ***Vocabulary Plus*** is a comprehensive online vocabulary program powered by TP's bestselling 9-book Vocabulary Series. *Vocabulary Plus* brings **all** the content of our famously clear, user-friendly texts directly to your tablet, smartphone, or computer. Offering traditional class-based approaches or an adaptive independent study mode, *Vocabulary Plus* can be purchased as an individual subscription, through an institutional license, or as part of a discounted textbook bundle. Contact Customer Service at cs@townsendpress.com or call (800) 772-6410 for purchase options. Two-week free trials are available!

Notes on the Fifth Edition

A number of enhancements have been made to the fifth edition of *Improving Vocabulary Skills, Short Version:*

- **An abundance of new and resequenced items.** As always, a good deal of content throughout the book has been replaced with brand new items to ensure the text works as clearly and effectively as possible with students. And items in both Sentence Checks have been resequenced from the previous edition. We listened to your requests!

- **Contemporary design.** Page format, design elements, and even the cover have been updated to reflect the vibrancy and energy of today's students and classrooms. While these visuals have been updated, the acclaimed clarity and readability of the previous editions have been preserved.

- **Thirty new photographs.** To engage today's visual learners, a full-color photograph has been added to the Final Check passage in each chapter.

- **General freshening for today's audiences.** The Vocabulary Series is popular in colleges as well as in middle and high schools. To reflect this diverse audience, practice materials, passages, and test items were freshened and updated for maximum appeal, relevance, and effectiveness for readers of all ages.

Acknowledgments

Having served as assistant editors for the Vocabulary Series for two decades, we are grateful to the mighty editorial crew at Townsend Press for their leadership, expertise, and patience. We stand on the shoulders of giants. Special gratitude goes to John Langan, Judy Nadell, Barbara Solot, Carole Mohr, and Sherrie L. Nist for their work on the book's previous editions. We would also like to thank Beth Johnson and Tanya Savory for their invaluable content contributions and Stéphane Descamps and Noémie Fior for the page design and layout of the fifth edition. A special shout-out goes to Bruce Kenselaar, who is responsible for the exciting new cover art and interior graphic design. Most of all, we continue to receive invaluable contributions from Janet Goldstein, editor extraordinaire, who has lent her exceptional and impeccable editing skills to this and so many Townsend Press publications. And a final tip of the hat goes to Anna, Sophia, and Yianni, our beloved budding wordsmiths.

Eliza Comodromos
Paul Langan

Introduction

Why Vocabulary Development Counts

You have probably often heard it said, "Building vocabulary is important." Maybe you've politely nodded in agreement and then forgotten the matter. But it would be fair for you to ask, "*Why* is vocabulary development important? Provide some evidence." Here are four compelling arguments:

1 Common sense tells you what many research studies have shown as well: vocabulary is a basic part of reading comprehension. Simply put, if you don't know enough words, you are going to have trouble understanding what you read. An occasional word may not stop you, but if there are too many words you don't know, comprehension will suffer. The content of textbooks is often challenging enough; you don't want to spend extra time on understanding the words that express that content.

2 Vocabulary is a major part of almost every standardized test, including reading achievement tests, high-school exit exams, college entrance exams, and armed forces and vocational placement tests. Test developers know that vocabulary is a key measure of both one's learning and one's ability to learn. It is for this reason that they include a separate vocabulary section as well as a reading comprehension section. The more words you know, then, the better you are likely to do on such important tests.

3 Studies have indicated that students with strong vocabularies are more successful in school. And one widely known study found that a good vocabulary, more than any other factor, was common to people enjoying successful careers in life. Words are, in fact, the tools not only of better reading, but of better writing, speaking, listening, and thinking as well. The more words you have at your command, the more effective your communication can be, and the more influence you can have on the people around you.

4 In today's world, a good vocabulary counts more than ever. Far fewer people work on farms or in factories. Far more are in jobs that provide services or process information. More than ever, words are the tools of our trade: words we use in reading, writing, listening, and speaking. Furthermore, experts say that tomorrow's workers will be called on to change jobs and learn new skills at an ever-increasing pace. The keys to survival and success will be the abilities to communicate skillfully and learn quickly. A solid vocabulary is essential for both of these skills.

Clearly, the evidence is overwhelming that building vocabulary is crucial. The question then becomes, "What is the best way of going about it?"

Words in Context: The Key to Vocabulary Development

Memorizing lists of words is a traditional method of vocabulary development. However, you are likely to forget such memorized lists quickly. Studies show that to master a word (or a word part), you must see and use it in various contexts. By working actively and repeatedly with a word, you greatly increase the chance of really learning it.

The following activity will make clear how this book is organized and how it uses a words-in-context approach. Answer the questions or fill in the missing words in the spaces provided.

Inside Front Cover and Contents

Turn to the inside front cover.

● The inside front cover provides a _____ that will help you pronounce all the vocabulary words in the book.

Now turn to the table of contents on pages v–vi.

● How many chapters are in the book? _____

● Four sections follow the last chapter. The first of these sections provides a limited answer key, the second gives helpful information on using _____, the third contains

_____, and the fourth is a list of the 200 words in the book.

Vocabulary Chapters

Turn to Chapter 1 on pages 8–11. This chapter, like all the others, consists of five parts:

● The *first part* of the chapter, on pages 8–9, is titled _____.

The left-hand column lists the ten words. Under each **boldfaced** word is its _____ (in parentheses). For example, the pronunciation of *absolve* is _____. For a guide to pronunciation, see the inside front cover as well as "Dictionary Use" on page 131.

Below the pronunciation guide for each word is its part of speech. The part of speech shown for *absolve* is _____. The vocabulary words in this book are mostly nouns, adjectives, and verbs. Nouns are words used to name something—a person, place, thing, or idea. Familiar nouns include *teacher, city, hat,* and *truth.* Adjectives are words that describe nouns, as in the following word pairs: *former* teacher, *large* city, *red* hat, *whole* truth. All of the verbs in this book express an action of some sort. They tell what someone or something is doing. Common verbs include *sing, separate, support,* and *imagine.*

To the right of each word are two sentences that will help you understand its meaning. In each sentence, the context—the words surrounding the boldfaced word—provides clues you can use to figure out the definition. There are four common types of context clues: examples, synonyms, antonyms, and the general sense of the sentence. Each is briefly described below.

1 Examples

A sentence may include examples that reveal what an unfamiliar word means. For instance, take a look at the following sentence from Chapter 1 for the word *eccentric*:

> Bruce is quite **eccentric**. For example, he lives in a circular house and rides to work on a motorcycle, in a three-piece suit.

The sentences provide two examples of what makes Bruce eccentric. The first is that he lives in a circular house. The second is that he rides to work on a motorcycle while wearing a three-piece suit. What do these two examples have in common? The answer to that question will tell you what *eccentric* means. Look at the answer choices below, and in the answer space provided, write the letter of the one you think is correct.

    ___ *Eccentric* means   A. ordinary.   B. odd.   C. careful.

Both of the examples given in the sentences about Bruce tell us that he is unusual, or odd. So if you wrote *B*, you chose the correct answer.

2 Synonyms

Synonyms are words that mean the same or almost the same as another word. For example, the words *joyful, happy,* and *delighted* are synonyms—they all mean about the same thing. Synonyms serve as context clues by providing the meaning of an unknown word that is nearby. The sentence below from Chapter 1 provides a synonym clue for *amiable.*

> At first, our history teacher doesn't seem very friendly, but once you get to know her, she shows her **amiable** side.

Instead of using *amiable* twice, the author used a synonym in the first part of the sentence. Find that synonym, and then choose the letter of the correct answer from the choices below.

    ___ *Amiable* means   A. intelligent.   B. uncaring.   C. good-natured.

The author uses two words to discuss one of the history teacher's qualities: *friendly* and *amiable.* This tells us that *amiable* must be another way of saying "friendly." (The author could have written, "she shows her friendly side.") Since *friendly* can also mean "good-natured," the correct answer is *C.*

3 Antonyms

Antonyms are words with opposite meanings. For example, *help* and *harm* are antonyms, as are *work* and *rest.* Antonyms serve as context clues by providing the opposite meaning of an unknown word. For instance, the sentence below from Chapter 1 provides an antonym clue for the word *antagonist.*

> In the ring, the two boxers were **antagonists,** but in their private lives, they were good friends.

The author is contrasting the boxers' two different relationships, so we can assume that *antagonists* and *good friends* have opposite, or contrasting, meanings. Using that contrast as a clue, write the letter of the answer that you think best defines *antagonist.*

    ___ *Antagonist* means   A. a supporter.   B. an enemy.   C. an example.

The correct answer is *B.* Because *antagonist* is the opposite of *friend*, it must mean "enemy."

4 General Sense of the Sentence

Even when there is no example, synonym, or antonym clue in a sentence, most of the time you can still figure out the meaning of an unfamiliar word. For example, look at the sentence from Chapter 1 for the word *malign.*

> That vicious Hollywood reporter often **maligns** movie stars, forever damaging their public images.

After studying the context carefully, you should be able to figure out what the reporter does to movie stars. That will be the meaning of *malign.* Write the letter of your choice.

    ___ *Malign* means   A. to praise.   B. to recognize.   C. to speak ill of.

Since the sentence calls the reporter "vicious" and says she damages public images, it is logical to conclude that she says negative things about movie stars. Thus answer *C* is correct.

By looking closely at the pair of sentences provided for each word, as well as the answer choices, you should be able to decide on the meaning of a word. As you figure out each meaning, you are working actively with the word. You are creating the groundwork you need to understand and to remember the word. *Getting involved with the word and developing a feel for it, based upon its use in context, is the key to word mastery.*

It is with good reason, then, that the directions at the top of page 8 tell you to use the context to figure out each word's _____. Doing so deepens your sense of the word and prepares you for the next activity.

● The **second part** of the chapter, on page 9, is titled _____.

According to research, it is not enough to see a word in context. At a certain point, it is helpful as well to see the meaning of a word. The matching activity provides that meaning, but it also makes you look for and think about that meaning. In other words, it continues the active learning that is your surest route to learning and remembering a word.

Note the caution that follows this activity. Do not proceed any further until you are sure that you know the correct meaning of each word as used in context.

Keep in mind that a word may have more than one meaning. In fact, some words have quite a few meanings. (If you doubt it, try looking up the word *make* or *draw* in a dictionary.) In this book, you will focus on one common meaning for each vocabulary word. However, many of the words have additional meanings. For example, in Chapter 9, you will learn that *devastate* means "to upset deeply," as in "Vera is so fond of Andy. She'll be **devastated** to hear he has cancer." If you then look up *devastate* in the dictionary, you will discover that it has another meaning—"to destroy," as in "The hurricane devastated much of Florida." After you learn one common meaning of a word, you will find yourself gradually learning its other meanings in the course of your academic and personal reading.

● The **third part** of the chapter, on page 10, is titled _____

Here are ten sentences that give you an opportunity to apply your understanding of the ten words. After inserting the words, check your answers in the limited answer key at the back of the book. Be sure to use the answer key as a learning tool only. Doing so will help you to master the words and to prepare for the last two activities and the unit tests, for which answers are not provided.

● The **fourth and fifth parts** of the chapter, on pages 10–11, are titled _____ and _____.

Each part tests you on all ten words, giving you two more chances to deepen your mastery. In the fifth part, you have the context of an entire passage in which you can practice applying the words.

At the bottom of the last page of this chapter is a box where you can enter your score for the final two checks. These scores should also be entered into the vocabulary performance chart located on the inside back cover of the book. To get your score, count the number of items that you answered correctly in each section. Then add a zero. For example, if you got seven answers right in Sentence Check 2, you would write "70" on the first line in the score box.

You now know, in a nutshell, how to proceed with the words in each chapter. Make sure that you do each page very carefully. *Remember that as you work through the activities, you are learning the words.*

How many times in all will you use each word? If you look, you'll see that each chapter gives you the opportunity to work with each word six times. Each "impression" adds to the likelihood that the word will become part of your active vocabulary. You will have further opportunities to use the word in the crossword puzzle and tests that end each unit and in the online exercises available at www.townsendpress.com.

In addition, many of the words are repeated in context in later chapters of the book. Such repeated words are marked with a small circle (°). For example, which words from Chapter 1 are repeated in the Final Check on page 15 of Chapter 2?

_____   _____

Analogies

This book also offers practice in word analogies, yet another way to deepen your understanding of words. An **analogy** is a similarity between two things that are otherwise different. Doing an analogy question is a two-step process. First you have to figure out the relationship in a pair of words. Those words are written like this:

LEAF : TREE

What is the relationship between the two words above? The answer can be stated like this: A leaf is a part of a tree.

Next, you must look for a similar relationship in a second pair of words. Here is how a complete analogy question looks:

LEAF : TREE ::

A. pond : river
B. foot : shoe

C. page : book
D. beach : sky

And here is how the question can be read:

___ LEAF is to TREE as

A. *pond* is to *river.*
B. *foot* is to *shoe.*

C. *page* is to *book.*
D. *beach* is to *sky.*

To answer the question, you have to decide which of the four choices has a relationship similar to the first one. Check your answer by seeing if it fits in the same wording as you used to show the relationship between *leaf* and *tree:* A ___ is part of a ___. Which answer do you choose?

The correct answer is *C.* Just as a leaf is part of a tree, a page is part of a book. On the other hand, a pond is not part of a river, nor is a foot part of a shoe, nor is a beach part of the sky.

We can state the complete analogy this way: *Leaf* is to *tree* as *page* is to *book.*

Here's another analogy question to try. Begin by figuring out the relationship between the first two words.

___ COWARD : HERO ::

A. soldier : military
B. infant : baby

C. actor : famous
D. employer : employee

Coward and *hero* are opposite types of people. So you need to look at the other four pairs to see which has a similar relationship. When you think you have found the answer, check to see that the two words you chose can be compared in the same way as *coward* and *hero:* ___ and ___ are opposite types of people.

In this case, the correct answer is *D; employer* and *employee* are opposite kinds of people. (In other words, *coward* is to *hero* as *employer* is to *employee.*)

By now you can see that there are basically two steps to doing analogy items:

1 Find out the relationship of the first two words.
2 Find the answer that expresses the same type of relationship as the first two words have.

Now try one more analogy question on your own. Write the letter of the answer you choose in the space provided.

___ SWING : BAT ::

A. drive : car
B. run : broom

C. catch : bat
D. fly : butterfly

If you chose answer *A,* you were right. *Swing* is what we do with a *bat,* and *drive* is what we do with a *car.*

Here are some other relationships often found in analogies:

- **Synonyms:** freedom : liberty (*freedom* and *liberty* mean the same thing)
- **Item to category:** baseball : sport (baseball is one kind of sport)
- **Item to description:** school bus : yellow (*yellow* is a word that describes a school bus)
- **Producer to product:** singer: song (a singer is the person who produces a song)
- **Time sequence:** January : March (January occurs two months before March)

A Final Thought

The facts are in. A strong vocabulary is a source of power. Words can make you a better reader, writer, speaker, thinker, and learner. They can dramatically increase your chances of success in school and in your job.

But words will not come automatically. They must be learned in a program of regular study. If you commit yourself to learning words, and you work actively and honestly with the chapters in this book, you will not only enrich your vocabulary—you will enrich your life as well.

Unit One

Chapter 1

- absolve
- adamant
- amiable
- amoral
- animosity
- antagonist
- eccentric
- encounter
- epitome
- malign

Chapter 2

- acclaim
- adjacent
- elicit
- engross
- escalate
- exploit
- methodical
- obsolete
- tangible
- terminate

Chapter 3

- allusion
- altruistic
- appease
- arbitrary
- assail
- banal
- euphemism
- mercenary
- syndrome
- taint

Chapter 4

- calamity
- comprehensive
- conventional
- flagrant
- fluctuate
- persevere
- ponder
- rehabilitate
- turmoil
- venture

Chapter 5

- attest
- attribute
- discern
- dispatch
- enhance
- enigma
- exemplify
- mobile
- nocturnal
- orient

CHAPTER 1

absolve	antagonist
adamant	eccentric
amiable	encounter
amoral	epitome
animosity	malign

Ten Words in Context

In the space provided, write the letter of the meaning closest to that of each **boldfaced** word. Use the context of the sentences to help you figure out each word's meaning.

1 absolve
(ăb-zŏlv´)
-verb

- Our dog, Rufus, was **absolved** of stealing Mom's glasses when they were found safe in her purse.
- Accused of taking bribes, the mayor said, "In the end, I'll clear my name and be **absolved** of any wrongdoing."

___ *Absolve* means   A. to accuse.   B. to clear of guilt.   C. to inform.

2 adamant
(ăd´ə-mənt)
-adjective

- Ron is **adamant** about not changing plans. He insists we should still camp out even though the weather report now says it will be cold and rainy.
- **Adamant** in his support of gun control, Senator Keen won't give in to pressure from powerful opponents.

___ *Adamant* means   A. firm.   B. uncertain.   C. flexible.

3 amiable
(ā´mē-ə-bəl)
-adjective

- My **amiable** dog greets both strangers and old friends with a happy yip and energetic tail-wagging.
- At first, our history teacher doesn't seem very friendly, but once you get to know her, she shows her **amiable** side.

___ *Amiable* means   A. intelligent.   B. uncaring.   C. good-natured.

4 amoral
(ā-mŏr´əl)
-adjective

- Jerry is almost totally **amoral**. He cares only about making money and having fun and couldn't care less about right or wrong.
- A former president of Uganda, Idi Amin, was truly **amoral**. He jailed, tortured, and killed innocent opponents without the slightest feeling of guilt.

___ *Amoral* means   A. cowardly.   B. lazy.   C. lacking ethical principles.

5 animosity
(ăn´ə-mŏs´ə-tē)
-noun

- The **animosity** between fans of the soccer teams was so strong that fights broke out all over the stadium.
- The bad feelings between the two families go back so many generations that nobody remembers what originally caused the **animosity**.

___ *Animosity* means   A. strong dislike.   B. admiration.   C. great fear.

6 antagonist
(ăn-tăg´ə-nĭst)
-noun

- At the divorce hearing, the husband and wife were such bitter **antagonists** that it was hard to believe they had once loved each other.
- In the ring, the two boxers were **antagonists**, but in their private lives, they were good friends.

___ *Antagonist* means   A. a supporter.   B. an enemy.   C. an example.

8

7 eccentric
(ĭk-sĕn′trĭk)
-adjective

- Bruce is quite **eccentric**. For example, he lives in a circular house and rides to work on a motorcycle, in a three-piece suit.
- Florence Nightingale, the famous nursing reformer, had the **eccentric** habit of carrying a pet owl around in one of her pockets.

___ *Eccentric* means   A. ordinary.   B. odd.   C. careful.

8 encounter
(ĕn-koun′tər)
-noun

- My **encounter** with Malik in a Los Angeles supermarket surprised me, since I thought he still lived in Chicago.
- I dislike returning to my small hometown, where I am likely to have **encounters** with people who knew me as a troubled kid.

___ *Encounter* means   A. a thought.   B. a dinner.   C. a meeting.

9 epitome
(ĭ-pĭt′ə-mē)
-noun

- To many, the **epitome** of cuteness is a furry, round-eyed puppy.
- The great ballplayer and civil rights leader Jackie Robinson was the **epitome** of both physical and moral strength.

___ *Epitome* means   A. a perfect model.   B. an opposite.   C. a main cause.

10 malign
(mə-līn′)
-verb

- That vicious Hollywood reporter often **maligns** movie stars, forever damaging their public images.
- Stacy refuses to **malign** her ex-husband, even though he was the one who insisted on the divorce.

___ *Malign* means   A. to praise.   B. to recognize.   C. to speak ill of.

Matching Words with Definitions

Following are definitions of the ten words. Clearly write or print each word next to its definition. The sentences above and on the previous page will help you decide on the meaning of each word.

1. _adamant_ — Not giving in; stubborn
2. _amoral_ — Lacking a moral sense; without principles
3. _eccentric_ — Differing from what is customary; odd
4. _absolve_ — To find innocent or blameless
5. _encounter_ — A brief or an unexpected meeting
6. _epitome_ — A perfect or typical example
7. _antagonist_ — An opponent; one who opposes or competes
8. _animosity_ — Bitter hostility
9. _malign_ — To make evil and often untrue statements about; speak evil of
10. _amicable_ — Good-natured; friendly and pleasant

CAUTION: Do not go any further until you are sure the above answers are correct. Then you can use the definitions to help you in the following practices. Your goal is eventually to know the words well enough so that you don't need to check the definitions at all.

Sentence Check 1

Using the answer line provided, complete each item below with the correct word from the box. Use each word once.

A. **absolve**	B. **adamant**	C. **amiable**	D. **amoral**	E. **animosity**
F. **antagonist**	G. **eccentric**	H. **encounter**	I. **epitome**	J. **malign**

amoral 1. Some criminals are truly ___—they don't see that some actions are right and that others are wrong.

amiable 2. Because he doesn't want to lose a sale, Mac remains polite and ___ even when he's annoyed with a customer.

malign 3. I'm tired of hearing the two candidates for governor ___ each other with stupid insults.

encounter 4. My brothers had planned to meet in the restaurant, but their ___ took place in the parking lot.

adamant 5. Lilly was ___ in her belief that Sam was a genius at business. Even after his first two companies failed, she still had faith in him.

eccentric 6. Today it's not odd for females to learn carpentry, but when my mother went to high school, girls who took wood shop were considered ___.

animosity 7. I avoid serious discussions with my sister because she shows great ___ toward me if I don't share her opinion.

antagonists 8. The owners of the department store were always competing with each other. They acted more like ___s than partners.

absolved 9. Jed was ___(e)d of stealing money from the company, but the damage the accusation did to his reputation remained.

epitome 10. The ___ of refreshment is drinking an ice-cold lemonade on a sizzling hot day.

NOTE: Now check your answers to these items by turning to page 129. Going over the answers carefully will help you prepare for the next two practices, for which answers are not given.

Sentence Check 2

Using the answer lines provided, complete each item below with **two** words from the box. Use each word once.

adamant
antagonist 1–2. Since the congresswoman was ___ in opposing the nuclear power plant, the plant's owners regarded her as their toughest ___.

animosity
malign 3–4. Hiroshi feels such ___ toward his sister that he never says a single kind thing about her; he only ___s her.

eccentric
_____ 5–6. The ___ millionaire dressed so shabbily that every ___ with him convinced us that he was poor.

_____ 7–8. With his friendly air, good-natured laugh and generosity, Santa Claus is the
_____   ___ of the ___ grandfather.

_____epitone_____ 9–10. Wayne is so ___ that he doesn't even want to be ___(e)d of guilt for all the
_____absolved_____   times he has lied, cheated, and stolen.

Final Check: *Joseph Palmer*

Here is a final opportunity for you to strengthen your knowledge of the ten words. First read the following selection carefully. Then fill in each blank with a word from the box at the top of the previous page. (Context clues will help you figure out which word goes in which blank.) Use each word once.

In 1830, a Massachusetts farmer named Joseph Palmer moved to the city, only to find that people continually reacted to him with anger and hatred. Why? Palmer certainly wasn't a(n) (1) animosty man—no, he had a strong sense of right and wrong. He was a friendly and (2) amicble person as well. And on the whole, Palmer was the (3) epitone of a normal citizen, living a typical life with his family. Yet his neighbors crossed to the other side of the street to avoid an (4) encounter with him. Children insulted Palmer and sometimes threw stones at him. Grown men hurled rocks through the windows of his house. Even the local minister (5) absolve malign (e)d Palmer, telling the congregation that Palmer admired only himself.

© Courtesy of The Trustees of Reservations, Archives, & Research Center.

One day, four men carrying scissors and a razor attacked Palmer and threw him to the ground. Pulling out a pocketknife, Palmer fought back, slashing at their legs. His (6) amoral s fled. Afterward, Palmer was the one arrested and jailed. While in jail, he was attacked two more times. Both times, he fought his way free. After a year—although his accusers still wouldn't (7) malign absolve him of guilt—he was released.

Palmer had won. The cause of all the (8) amoral animosty and abuse had been his long, flowing beard. Palmer, (9) adamont to the end, had refused to shave.

Thirty years after Palmer's difficulties, it was no longer considered (10) arresvic to wear whiskers. Among the many who wore beards then was the President of the United States, Abraham Lincoln.

| Scores | Sentence Check 2 _____% | Final Check _____% |

Enter your scores above and in the **Vocabulary Performance Chart** on the inside back cover of the book.

acclaim	exploit
adjacent	methodical
elicit	obsolete
engross	tangible
escalate	terminate

Ten Words in Context

In the space provided, write the letter of the meaning closest to that of each **boldfaced** word. Use the context of the sentences to help you figure out each word's meaning.

1 acclaim
(ə-klām′)
-noun

- Any subway system that is clean, quiet, and safe deserves **acclaim**.
- Although Vincent Van Gogh's paintings are now worth millions of dollars, the artist received little **acclaim** in his lifetime and died in poverty.

___ *Acclaim* means   A. criticism.   B. praise.   C. change.

2 adjacent
(ə-jā′sənt)
-adjective

- Because their desks are **adjacent**, Jeff and Kellie often exchange looks and comments.
- If you keep your dishes in a cupboard that's **adjacent** to the dishwasher, you won't have to walk too far when putting away the clean dishes.

___ *Adjacent* means   A. close.   B. similar.   C. separated.

3 elicit
(ĭ-lĭs′ĭt)
-verb

- The movie star's violet eyes always **elicit** admiration and wonder.
- The basketball player's three-point shot to win the game in its final seconds **elicited** a roar of delight from the excited fans.

___ *Elicit* means   A. to stop.   B. to follow.   C. to bring out.

4 engross
(ĕn′grōs′)
-verb

- The suspenseful TV movie so **engrossed** Bryan that he didn't even budge when he was called to dinner.
- The fascinating single-file march of black ants along the sidewalk **engrossed** me for several minutes.

___ *Engross* means   A. to hold the interest of.   B. to disgust.   C. to bore.

5 escalate
(ĕs′kə-lāt′)
-verb

- The fight between the two hockey players **escalated** into an all-out battle among members of both teams.
- "We need to **escalate** our fund-raising efforts," the theater manager said. "Otherwise, the company won't survive."

___ *Escalate* means   A. to expand.   B. to delay.   C. to weaken.

6 exploit
(ĕks-ploit′)
-verb

- At the turn of the century, factory owners **exploited** children by making them work in terrible conditions for as many as eighteen hours a day.
- Although Ricky is the English teacher's son, he refuses to **exploit** his status. He works as hard as anyone else in the class.

___ *Exploit* means   A. to forget.   B. to take advantage of.   C. to be sad about.

7 methodical
(mə-thŏd′ĭ-kəl)
-adjective

● A **methodical** way to store spices is to shelve them in alphabetical order.
● Juanita is so **methodical** about her diet that she classifies the foods in each meal into different nutritional categories.

___ *Methodical* means   A. accidental.   B. out-of-date.   ✓C. orderly.

8 obsolete
(ŏb′sə-lēt′)
-adjective

● Smartphones are so common now that they have made pagers **obsolete**.
● Printed books may one day become **obsolete** as more people choose to read on electronic devices.

___ *Obsolete* means   A. popular.   B. useful.   C. extinct.

9 tangible
(tăn′jə-bəl)
-adjective

● The sculptor loved making her ideas **tangible** by giving them form in metal and stone.
● Corn-chip crumbs, empty soda bottles, and dirty napkins were **tangible** evidence that a party had taken place the night before.

___ *Tangible* means   A. clever.   B. solid.   C. hidden.

10 terminate
(tûr′mə-nāt′)
-verb

● As the clock's hands inched toward 3:00, the students waited impatiently for the bell to **terminate** the last class before spring vacation.
● The referee should have **terminated** the boxing match when he first saw the weaker fighter losing the ability to defend himself.

___ *Terminate* means   A. to end.   B. to revive.   C. to begin.

Matching Words with Definitions

Following are definitions of the ten words. Clearly write or print each word next to its definition. The sentences above and on the previous page will help you decide on the meaning of each word.

1. _elict_____ To draw forth
2. _terminate_____ To stop; bring to an end
3. _methodical_____ Orderly; systematic
4. _adjacent_____ Close; near (to something)
5. _tangible_____ Able to be touched; having form and matter
6. _obsolete_____ No longer active or in use; out of date
7. _escalate_____ To increase or intensify
8. _acclaim_____ Great praise or applause; enthusiastic approval
9. _engross_____ To hold the full attention of; absorb
10. _exploit_____ To use selfishly or unethically; take unfair advantage of

CAUTION: Do not go any further until you are sure the above answers are correct. Then you can use the definitions to help you in the following practices. Your goal is eventually to know the words well enough so that you don't need to check the definitions at all.

Sentence Check 1

Using the answer line provided, complete each item below with the correct word from the box. Use each word once.

A. **acclaim**	B. **adjacent**	C. **elicit**	D. **engross**	E. **escalate**
F. **exploit**	G. **methodical**	H. **obsolete**	I. **tangible**	J. **terminate**

elict 1. The shouting match between Rose and her brother ___(e)d until it was so loud that the neighbors complained.

adjacent 2. Our house is ___ to one with a high wooden fence, so our view on that side is completely blocked.

acclaim 3. With movies like *Saving Private Ryan, Forrest Gump, Cast Away,* and *Charlie Wilson's War* to his credit, actor Tom Hanks has won Oscars and the ___ of admiring critics.

obsolete 4. A typical office of the 1960s contained objects that are ___ today, such as typewriters and adding machines.

tangible 5. A wedding ring is a(n) ___ expression of a couple's commitment to each other.

engross 6. In one disturbing survey, the question "Which do you like better, TV or Daddy?" ___(e)d this response from a number of children: "TV."

terminate 7. When Luke was caught stealing money on the job, the company ___(e)d his employment and brought him up on criminal charges.

methodical 8. Diana is very ___ when it comes to cooking. She reads the recipe carefully, gathers all the ingredients, and gets out the utensils before beginning.

exploit 9. When workers feel ___(e)d by their employers, they often go on strike for larger salaries and better working conditions.

escalate 10. Sometimes an article I'm reading on the bus will ___ me so much that I'll pass my stop.

NOTE: Now check your answers to these items by turning to page 129. Going over the answers carefully will help you prepare for the next two practices, for which answers are not given.

Sentence Check 2

Using the answer lines provided, complete each item below with **two** words from the box. Use each word once.

escalate tangible
exploit acclaim 1-2. Workers want ___ rewards such as a good salary and a health-care program, but they also welcome less concrete benefits, such as ___ for a job well done.

obsolete
terminate 3-4. Although hand-crafted furniture is almost ___, mass production hasn't yet ___(e)d all demand for it.

engross
acclaim
eliot 5-6. The gifted ice skater's routine ___(e)d the audience. It was the epitome° of grace and power combined. At the end, a long, rapid spin ___(e)d a burst of applause.

acclaim

adjacent

exploit

escalate

7–8. Patty's ___ approach to gardening is to arrange all the plants in a row, with each one ___ to the one that will be planted after it.

9–10. The more the British ___(e)d the American colonies by taxing them unfairly, the more the colonists' animosity° toward the British ___(e)d.

Final Check: *Death of the Big Top*

Here is a final opportunity for you to strengthen your knowledge of the ten words. First read the following selection carefully. Then fill in each blank with a word from the box at the top of the previous page. (Context clues will help you figure out which word goes in which blank.) Use each word once.

For generations, the traveling circus was a part of the American landscape. The excitement would begin with the arrival of a caravan of trucks loaded with freakish performers and unusual animals. Crowds from (1) adjacent towns would gather, (2) engross (e)d by the sight of workers putting up "The Big Top"—the tent that housed the performance. "When are you going?" would be the question on everyone's lips. No one would think of missing such a show!

But today, few traveling circuses exist. They have disappeared for several reasons. First of all, entertainment is everywhere today. With multiplex cinemas, wide-screen TVs, on-demand shows, social media, and YouTube, people don't need to go to the circus for amusement. Compared to other forms of entertainment, a tightrope walker or a clown in "The Big Top" seems old-fashioned.

Another reason for the decline of circuses is the growing concerns about how circuses (3) exploit animals. While the sight of elephants standing on their hind legs or tigers jumping through fiery hoops once (4) elicit (e)d cheers and other expressions of (5) acclaim , today's audiences care about the welfare of animals. Too often, circus animals were put through strict, (6) methodical "training" that also included being beaten, frightened, and starved to make them perform. Furthermore, the animals were forced to live in cramped cages as they traveled from one town to another.

For years, animal rights groups worked to (7) terminate these practices, which they consider amoral°. Using such tools as secret cameras, they produced (8) tangible evidence of abuse, such as photographs of wounds on animals. In response, adamant° protests against animal cruelty (9) escalate. (e)d, and circus crowds grew smaller. Fewer people were willing to attend performances.

Although traveling circuses were a colorful part of America's history, they are becoming (10) obsolete . From the animals' point of view, that is a good thing.

Scores   Sentence Check 2 _____%   Final Check _____%

allusion	banal
altruistic	euphemism
appease	mercenary
arbitrary	syndrome
assail	taint

Ten Words in Context

In the space provided, write the letter of the meaning closest to that of each **boldfaced** word. Use the context of the sentences to help you figure out each word's meaning.

1 allusion
(ə-lōō′zhən)
-*noun*

● After I suggested that Monty have fruit for dessert instead of chocolate cake, he responded, "Is that an **allusion** to my weight?"

● Ramon didn't have the courage to come right out and ask Lia to marry him. Instead, he made only an **allusion** to marriage by asking, "Wouldn't it be easier if we had to fill out just one tax return?"

___ *Allusion to* means   A. a contrast to.   B. a hint about.   C. an answer for.

2 altruistic
(ăl′trōō-ĭs′tĭk)
-*adjective*

● When an enemy approaches, ground squirrels show **altruistic** behavior. They risk their own lives to give alarm calls to nearby relatives.

● "I'm not often **altruistic**," Brett admitted. "I usually put my own welfare first."

___ *Altruistic* means   A. unselfish.   B. cheerful.   C. greedy.

3 appease
(ə-pēz′)
-*verb*

● The elderly woman was able to **appease** the fussy baby by singing him a gentle lullaby.

● Roger was furious when he saw me out with another guy, but I quickly **appeased** him by explaining that the "date" was my cousin.

___ *Appease* means   A. to annoy.   B. to heal.   C. to calm.

4 arbitrary
(är′bĭ-trĕr′ē)
-*adjective*

● Professor Miller's students were angry that he graded essays in an **arbitrary** way, rather than using clear-cut standards.

● Parents should not enforce rules according to their moods. Such **arbitrary** discipline only confuses children.

___ *Arbitrary* means   A. steady.   B. slow.   C. impulsive.

5 assail
(ə-sāl′)
-*verb*

● The storm **assailed** us with hail and heavy rain.

● The two candidates continuously **assailed** each other with accusations of dishonesty.

___ *Assail* means   A. to attack.   B. to confuse.   C. to support.

6 banal
(bə-năl′)
-*adjective*

● The film, with its repetitive conversations and unimaginative plot, was the most **banal** I had ever seen.

● "Nice to see you" may be a **banal** comment, but what it lacks in originality it makes up for in friendliness.

___ *Banal* means   A. greedy.   B. unoriginal.   C. clever.

7 euphemism
(yo͞o′fə-mĭz′əm)
-*noun*

- Common **euphemisms** include "final resting place" (for *grave*), "intoxicated" (for *drunk*), and "powder room" (for *toilet*).
- The Central Intelligence Agency is on record as having referred to assassination with the **euphemism** "change of health."

__ *Euphemism* means   A. a harsh term.   B. a term that doesn't offend.   C. a foreign term.

8 mercenary
(mûr′sə-nĕr′ē)
-*adjective*

- Ed is totally **mercenary**. His philosophy is, "Pay me enough, and I'll do anything."
- The con man pretended to love the wealthy widow, but he actually married her for **mercenary** reasons.

__ *Mercenary* means   A. jealous.   B. angry.   C. greedy.

9 syndrome
(sĭn′drōm)
-*noun*

- Headaches are usually harmless, but as part of a **syndrome** including fever and a stiff neck, they may be a sign of a serious illness.
- Jet lag is a **syndrome** resulting from flying long distances; it often includes exhaustion, headache, and loss of appetite.

__ *Syndrome* means   A. a group of symptoms.   B. a cause.   C. something required.

10 taint
(tānt)
-*verb*

- The involvement of organized crime has **tainted** many sports, including boxing and horse racing.
- The government scandal **tainted** the reputations of everyone involved.

__ *Taint* means   A. to benefit.   B. to damage.   C. to start.

Matching Words with Definitions

Following are definitions of the ten words. Clearly write or print each word next to its definition. The sentences above and on the previous page will help you decide on the meaning of each word.

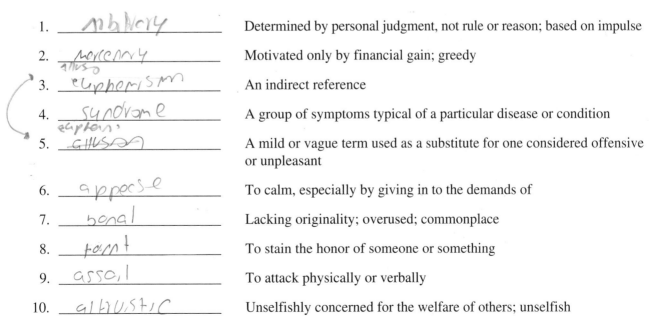

1. _____arbitrary_____   Determined by personal judgment, not rule or reason; based on impulse

2. _____mercenary_____   Motivated only by financial gain; greedy

3. _____euphemism_____   An indirect reference

4. _____syndrome_____   A group of symptoms typical of a particular disease or condition

5. _____cliché_____   A mild or vague term used as a substitute for one considered offensive or unpleasant

6. _____appease_____   To calm, especially by giving in to the demands of

7. _____banal_____   Lacking originality; overused; commonplace

8. _____taint_____   To stain the honor of someone or something

9. _____assail_____   To attack physically or verbally

10. _____altruistic_____   Unselfishly concerned for the welfare of others; unselfish

CAUTION: Do not go any further until you are sure the above answers are correct. Then you can use the definitions to help you in the following practices. Your goal is eventually to know the words well enough so that you don't need to check the definitions at all.

Sentence Check 1

Using the answer line provided, complete each item below with the correct word from the box. Use each word once.

A. allusion	B. altruistic	C. appease	D. arbitrary	E. assail
F. banal	G. euphemism	H. mercenary	I. syndrome	J. taint

euphemis 1. When the word "died" seems too harsh, people use the ___s "passed away" or "is at peace."

assail 2. The prankster ___(e)d his victims by squirting them with honey and then showering them with flour.

altruistic 3. Jayden is so ___, he decided to spend his vacation rebuilding homes damaged by the hurricane.

allusion 4. "Someone hasn't shown me her report card," my mother said, making a(n) ___ to my sister.

mercenary 5. My brother is so ___, I think he'd sell our grandmother if the price was right.

banal 6. "You're special" probably appears on thousands of greeting cards, but when someone says it to you and means it, it never seems ___.

arbitrary 7. The judge's harsh sentence was ___. Rather than being based on past similar cases or on the seriousness of the crime, it was based on the judge's opinion of the defendant.

syndrome 8. Abraham Lincoln is thought to have had Marfan's ___, a group of symptoms which includes unusually long bones and abnormal blood circulation.

appease 9. The only thing that will ___ angry parents in our community is firing the coach accused of stealing team funds.

taint 10. The report that the halfback was addicted to drugs ___(e)d the team's image.

NOTE: Now check your answers to these items by turning to page 129. Going over the answers carefully will help you prepare for the next two practices, for which answers are not given.

Sentence Check 2

Using the answer lines provided, complete each item below with **two** words from the box. Use each word once.

arbitrary
euphemism 1–2. My boss judges performance in a(n) ___ manner, praising and scolding according to his moods. And when he says, "Please stay a few minutes longer today," "a few minutes" is a(n) ___ for "an hour."

syndrome
taint 3–4. A certain rare ___ includes a very odd symptom—an uncontrollable urge to use obscene language. This disease can ___ a victim's reputation, because some people who hear the foul language won't understand the reason for it.

assail
appease 5–6. The angry customer loudly ___(e)d the salesman for having sold her a broken clock. The salesman quickly ___(e)d her by giving her a full refund.

altruistic
mercenary 7–8. ___ people tend to place the public welfare above their own self-interest. In contrast, ___ people will exploit° anyone for a profit—they will even sell harmful products.

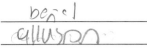

_____banal_____

_____allusion·_____   9–10. The critic hated stale language. Instead of writing a(n) ___ comment such as "That ballerina is light on her feet," he made an interesting ___ to the dancer's movements: "She was never heavier than moonlight."

Final Check: *No Luck with Women*

Here is a final opportunity for you to strengthen your knowledge of the ten words. First read the following selection carefully. Then fill in each blank with a word from the box at the top of the previous page. (Context clues will help you figure out which word goes in which blank.) Use each word once.

My older brother, Mark, has no luck with women. He doesn't understand why. I do.

To begin with, when he first meets a woman, he goes into one of two styles of conversation. The first is to (1)_essail_____ her with a stream of personal questions: "What's your name? Where do you live? Is that your real hair color? What kind of work do you do? Do you want to have kids someday? Are you seeing anyone? Would you like to have dinner with me?" Naturally, most women find this surprising and annoying. His other approach is to say the most (2)_____banal__ things imaginable: "Nice day, isn't it? I thought it might rain this morning, but it didn't. It might rain tomorrow, but who knows. Last week was nice weather, too." By this time, the poor girl has either walked away or passed out from boredom.

Another thing Mark often does in his encounters° with women is to say things that make him sound totally (3)_mercenary_____, as if money were the most important thing in the world to him. He makes frequent (4)_allusion·_____s to his own salary, asks the woman how much she makes, and complains about the prices of everything on a menu. When he takes a date to a movie, he sometimes embarrasses her by trying to get his money back from the theater manager afterward, claiming he hadn't liked the movie. Naturally, this sort of behavior somewhat (5)_taint_____s him in the woman's eyes, and he rarely gets a second date. When one of his former girlfriends complained to me about Mark's behavior, I tried to (6)_appease_____ her by telling her that underneath it all, Mark is really a nice guy. She replied by saying that she didn't have the desire to dig that far down.

Mark, of course, finds women's reactions to him completely (7)_arbitrary_____. He shakes his head and says, "Women are just not reasonable. Here I am, as nice as can be, and they act as if I have some horrible, contagious (8)_syndrome_____." I try to be a(n) (9)_altruistic_____ sister and help the guy out. I point out how his behaviors turn women off, using gentle (10)_euphemism_____s such as "You're a special, unusual person, Mark. You're just a little eccentric°." Maybe I need to come right out and let him hear the truth, even if it makes him mad: "You're *weird*, Mark."

Scores   Sentence Check 2 _____%   Final Check _____%

calamity	persevere
comprehensive	ponder
conventional	rehabilitate
flagrant	turmoil
fluctuate	venture

Ten Words in Context

In the space provided, write the letter of the meaning closest to that of each **boldfaced** word. Use the context of the sentences to help you figure out each word's meaning.

1 calamity
(kə-lăm′ĭ-tē)
-noun

● The survivors of the earthquake slowly rebuilt their homes and lives after the **calamity**.

● Our neighbor's house burned down one night in May. Ever since that **calamity**, some of the children on our street have been afraid to go to bed at night.

___ *Calamity* means   A. an activity.   B. a tragedy.   C. a risk.

2 comprehensive
(kŏm′prē-hĕn′sĭv)
-adjective

● That article on sightseeing in Charleston was not **comprehensive**. It failed to mention many points of interest in that wonderful city.

● The company's **comprehensive** insurance plan covers most health services, including hospitals, doctors, and dentists.

___ *Comprehensive* means   A. complete.   B. familiar.   C. continuous.

3 conventional
(kən-vĕn′shə-nəl)
-adjective

● Two **conventional** Valentine's Day gifts are roses and chocolates.

● Jorge wanted to propose to Ramona in the **conventional** manner, so in the middle of a restaurant, he got down on one knee and asked, "Will you marry me?"

___ *Conventional* means   A. out-of-the-way.   B. useful.   C. usual.

4 flagrant
(flā′grənt)
-adjective

● The use of campaign funds for the congressman's private business was a **flagrant** violation of the law.

● In **flagrant** disregard of his parents' stated wishes, Art wore a T-shirt and jeans to their dinner party.

___ *Flagrant* means   A. obvious.   B. acceptable.   C. minor.

5 fluctuate
(flŭk′chōō-āt′)
-verb

● My weight used to **fluctuate** between 150 and 190 pounds. Now it's steady, at 170 pounds.

● Desert temperatures can **fluctuate** by as much as fifty degrees between daytime and nighttime.

___ *Fluctuate* means   A. to continue.   B. to vary.   C. to follow.

6 persevere
(pûr′sə-vîr′)
-verb

● "I know you're tired," Jack said, "but we've got to **persevere** and get to the camp before the storm hits."

● It was not easy to attend English classes while working at two jobs, but Nina **persevered** until she could speak English well.

___ *Persevere* means   A. to surrender.   B. to hold back.   C. to keep going.

7 ponder
(pŏn′dər)
-*verb*

- Too often we don't take time to **ponder** the possible consequences of our actions.
- Over the years, Mr. Madigan rarely took time to **ponder** the meaning of life. Since his heart attack, however, he's thought a lot about what is important to him.

___ *Ponder* means   A. to wait for.   B. to ignore.   C. to think about.

8 rehabilitate
(rē′hə-bĭl′ə-tāt)
-*verb*

- Most prisons make little effort to **rehabilitate** inmates so that they can lead productive, wholesome lives after their release.
- My grandfather learned to walk, write, and speak again in a program that **rehabilitates** stroke victims.

___ *Rehabilitate* means   A. to pay back.   B. to return to normal life.   C. to depend upon.

9 turmoil
(tûr′moil)
-*noun*

- Without a teacher, the sixth-grade class was in **turmoil**, until the principal entered the room and the students quickly came to order.
- After the **turmoil** of crying babies, active children, and trying to feed 120 people, I'm glad when our family reunions end.

___ *Turmoil* means   A. discussion.   B. disorder.   C. harmony.

10 venture
(vĕn′chər)
-*verb*

- "I'll **venture** going on any ride in this amusement park except the Twister," said Nick. "I'll risk getting sick to my stomach, but I won't risk my life."
- "At tomorrow's staff meeting," my older sister said, "I will **venture** to say what I really think—and cross my fingers that I don't get fired."

___ *Venture* means   A. to dare.   B. to remember.   C. to imagine.

Matching Words with Definitions

Following are definitions of the ten words. Clearly write or print each word next to its definition. The sentences above and on the previous page will help you decide on the meaning of each word.

1. ___flagrant___   Shockingly obvious; outrageous

2. ___venture___   To take the risk of; dare

3. ___comprehesive___   Including all or much

4. ___rehabilitate___   To restore to a normal life through therapy or education

5. ___persevere___   To continue with an effort or plan despite difficulties

6. ___turmoil___   Complete confusion; uproar

7. ___calamity___   An event bringing great loss and misery

8. ___fluctuate___   To vary irregularly; to go up and down or back and forth

9. ___ponder___   To consider carefully; think deeply about

10. ___conventional___   Customary; ordinary

CAUTION: Do not go any further until you are sure the above answers are correct. Then you can use the definitions to help you in the following practices. Your goal is eventually to know the words well enough so that you don't need to check the definitions at all.

Sentence Check 1

Using the answer line provided, complete each item below with the correct word from the box. Use each word once.

A. calamity	B. comprehensive	C. conventional	D. flagrant	E. fluctuate
F. persevere	G. ponder	H. rehabilitate	I. turmoil	J. venture

comprehesue   1. Nobody in Doug's family has a ___ job. His mother is a drummer, his father is a magician, and his uncle is a wine taster.

conventoncl   2. Our history exam will be ___; it will cover everything we've studied since September.

flegrant   3. When Charlene lost her job because she spoke up for a fellow employee, it was a ___ violation of her rights.

ponaer   4. Some people have a child without taking time to ___ parenthood. They give less thought to having a baby than to buying a sofa.

calomty   5. Tracy is so vain that she considers it a ___ if a pimple appears anywhere on her face.

ue ttue   6. Instead of hiring a lawyer, the defendant will ___ to plead her own case in court.

fluctucle   7. The way my dog's appetite ____(e)d this week worries me. One day she hardly ate anything, and the next day she gulped down everything I gave her.

turmoil   8. The day we moved, the apartment was in ___. Boxes and people were everywhere, and the baby wouldn't stop crying.

rehcbilitcle   9. It took many months of therapy to ___ my aunt after she lost her sight, but now she can get around her home and neighborhood on her own.

persevere   10. Learning the new software program was difficult, but when Maria saw how useful it would be in her work, she was glad she had ___(e)d.

NOTE: Now check your answers to these items by turning to page 129. Going over the answers carefully will help you prepare for the next two practices, for which answers are not given.

Sentence Check 2

Using the answer lines provided, complete each item below with **two** words from the box. Use each word once.

conventoncl
flegrant   1–2. When he drives alone, Marshall's behavior is very ___; he obeys all the traffic rules. But when his friends are with him, he shows off with ___ violations of the speed limit.

rehabilcle
perscruve   3–4. A drug-treatment center can ___ most addicts. Among the failures are addicts who don't ___ with the treatment and leave the center early.

ventue
colomty   5–6. The one time my cousin ___(e)d skydiving, the result was a ___. Her parachute didn't open, and she was injured so badly in the fall that she almost died.

_____

_____   7–8. The boss's moods and orders ___ so wildly at times that they throw the department into ___. As a result, productivity is at an all-time low, and it will take a new boss to revitalize° this office.

_____   9–10. "We need to ___ all we might do to help families in trouble," said the social
comprehensive   worker to her staff. "We must plan a ___ program, not just a narrow plan dealing with only one part of their lives."

Final Check: *Accident and Recovery*

Here is a final opportunity for you to strengthen your knowledge of the ten words. First read the following selection carefully. Then fill in each blank with a word from the box at the top of the previous page. (Context clues will help you figure out which word goes in which blank.) Use each word once.

We tried to stop Rosa from jumping, but her (1)_____*impulsive*_____ disregard of our warnings led to a (2)_____*calamity*_____ that would change her life forever. She dove off a rock into a river none of us was sure was deep enough. When she hit the bottom, she broke her back.

I visited Rosa at the hospital every day for the next few weeks. I saw her mood (3)_____*conventional*_____ between anger and quiet depression. Her whole life seemed in (4)_____; she was too confused and shaken up to think reasonably about her future.

Within about a month, however, I began to see a change in Rosa. She had moved to Henner House to participate in a very (5)_____*comprehensive*_____ program, designed to meet all the needs of patients like Rosa. The program (6)_____*rehabilitate*_____s accident victims so that they can subsequently return to fulfilling lives. Rosa gained hope once she saw she could learn to do such everyday tasks as cooking, cleaning, and bathing. After learning how to get around indoors, she (7)_____*venture*_____(e)d traveling around the city in her wheelchair. The more she did, the better she felt. The staff also helped Rosa plan for her future. They urged her to (8)_____*ponder*_____ her goals and how she might meet them. At times, it was difficult for her to (9)_____*persevere*_____ with the program, but she didn't quit.

Now, ten months later, Rosa is able to live a somewhat (10)_____ life. Her disability is not a roadblock; she is able to do many of the ordinary things she used to do—work, drive, and live in an apartment with a friend. Yes, her life has changed forever. But Rosa is once again glad to be alive.

Scores   Sentence Check 2 _____%   Final Check _____%

attest	enigma
attribute	exemplify
discern	mobile
dispatch	nocturnal
enhance	orient

Ten Words in Context

In the space provided, write the letter of the meaning closest to that of each **boldfaced** word. Use the context of the sentences to help you figure out each word's meaning.

1 attest
(ə-tĕst′)
-*verb*

● Anyone who has seen the Golden Gate Bridge in the rose-gold light of sunset can **attest** to its beauty.

● Witnesses **attest** to the fact that rainfall makes the ground of Death Valley so slippery that boulders slide across it.

___ *Attest to* means   A. to declare to be true.   B. to wish for.   C. to forget easily.

2 attribute
(ăt′rə-byōōt′)
-*noun*

● A three-hundred-page novel written in 1939 has the odd **attribute** of containing no *e*, the most common letter in English.

● Some cars have computerized **attributes** such as windshield wipers that automatically turn on when it rains.

___ *Attribute* means   A. a tendency.   B. a defect.   C. a characteristic.

3 discern
(dĭ-sûrn′)
-*verb*

● An experienced jeweler can easily **discern** whether a diamond is genuine or fake.

● People who are red-green colorblind can **discern** the colors of traffic lights by recognizing shades of gray.

___ *Discern* means   A. to see clearly.   B. to disregard.   C. to change.

4 dispatch
(dĭ-spăch′)
-*verb*

● I wanted to **dispatch** the letter as quickly as possible, so I took it to the post office instead of dropping it into a mailbox.

● At work Harold is treated like an errand boy. His boss often **dispatches** him to the deli for sandwiches or donuts.

___ *Dispatch* means   A. to represent.   B. to send.   C. to drive.

5 enhance
(ĕn-hăns′)
-*verb*

● Our gym teacher **enhanced** her appearance with a more attractive hairstyle.

● The college catalogue stated that the writing course would "**enhance** all students' writing skills" by improving their grammar and style.

___ *Enhance* means   A. to make better.   B. to recognize.   C. to reduce.

6 enigma
(ĭ-nĭg′mə)
-*noun*

● How the thief entered our house was an **enigma** until we remembered that the cellar door had been left unlocked.

● The "singing sands" of Scotland remained an **enigma** until scientists learned that footsteps caused the round grains of sand and the surrounding air pockets to make musical vibrations.

___ *Enigma* means   A. a comfort.   B. a puzzle.   C. an error.

7 exemplify
(ĭg-zĕm′plə-fī′)
-verb

- Mr. Whiskers **exemplifies** everything I love about cats. He's smart, lazy, and unconcerned about humans.
- Mr. Ramirez, who emphasizes original thinking and freedom of expression, **exemplifies** the best in teaching.

__ *Exemplify* means   A. to illustrate.   B. to save.   C. to oppose.

8 mobile
(mō′bəl)
-adjective

- My parents own a **mobile** home, which can be moved from place to place.
- Every morning when I was in the hospital, a volunteer wheeled a **mobile** library into my room.

__ *Mobile* means   A. active.   B. expensive.   C. movable.

9 nocturnal
(nŏk-tûr′nəl)
-adjective

- I know when my brother has enjoyed one of his **nocturnal** feasts because I find a stack of dishes in the sink in the morning.
- Since owls are **nocturnal**, they are rarely seen during the day.

__ *Nocturnal* means   A. noisy.   B. busy.   C. of the night.

10 orient
(ôr′ē-ĕnt)
-verb

- When coming up from the subway, I often need to look at a street sign to **orient** myself.
- GPS apps and smartphones have made travel easier by helping people **orient** themselves in unfamiliar places.

__ *Orient* means   A. to locate.   B. to welcome.   C. to question.

Matching Words with Definitions

Following are definitions of the ten words. Clearly write or print each word next to its definition. The sentences above and on the previous page will help you decide on the meaning of each word.

1. ___enigma___   A mystery or puzzle

2. ___dspatcn___   To send to a specific place or on specific business

3. ___nocturnal___   Of, about, or happening in the night; active at night

4. ___attest___   To make a statement about something on the basis of personal experience; bear witness; testify

5. ___orent___   To determine one's location or direction; to locate in relation to a direction (east, west, etc.)

6. ___dscovn___   To recognize; detect

7. ___enhonce___   To improve; add to the strength, beauty, or value of something

8. ___mobile___   Moving or able to move from place to place

9. ___attribute___   A quality or feature of a person or thing

10. ___exemplify___   To be an example of; represent; be typical of

CAUTION: Do not go any further until you are sure the above answers are correct. Then you can use the definitions to help you in the following practices. Your goal is eventually to know the words well enough so that you don't need to check the definitions at all.

Sentence Check 1

Using the answer line provided, complete each item below with the correct word from the box. Use each word once.

A. **attest**	B. **attribute**	C. **discern**	D. **dispatch**	E. **enhance**
F. **enigma**	G. **exemplify**	H. **mobile**	I. **nocturnal**	J. **orient**

enigma 1. Science does not have enough evidence to solve the ___ of whether or not there is other intelligent life in the universe.

exemplify 2. The lives of such reformers as Susan B. Anthony, Mahatma Gandhi, and Martin Luther King ___ greatness.

dispach 3. When I was younger, my mother used to ___ me to the store for milk or some missing cooking ingredient as often as twice a day.

attest 4. A witness ___(e)d to the truth of the defendant's claim that she had loved the murdered man.

enhance 5. Fresh garlic may not ___ the breath, but it certainly improves spaghetti sauce.

attributes 6. Giant kelp, a form of seaweed, has some amazing ___s. Not only is it the world's fastest-growing vegetable, but the more it is cut, the faster it grows.

mobile 7. My mother is unable to walk, but with her wheelchair she is ___ enough to get around her apartment, move along a sidewalk, and even shop at a mall.

orient 8. The positions of the stars help sailors ___ themselves on the open seas.

discern 9. Sue's hairpiece is so natural-looking that it's impossible to ___ where the hairpiece ends and her own hair begins.

nocturnal 10. The convicts decided on a(n) ___ escape. The darkness would hide them as they fled through the forest.

NOTE: Now check your answers to these items by turning to page 129. Going over the answers carefully will help you prepare for the next two practices, for which answers are not given.

Sentence Check 2

Using the answer lines provided, complete each item below with **two** words from the box. Use each word once.

attributes
exemplify
1–2. In fables, animals often illustrate human ___s. In the story of the race between the tortoise and the hare, the tortoise is meant to ___ the human qualities of being slow but steady. Despite competing against a much speedier antagonist°, he perseveres° and defeats the overly confident hare.

moble
_____
3–4. A ___ robot that collects and delivers mail throughout the office building ___s itself with electric eyes.

_____
_____
5–6. Because Helen Keller could not hear or see, the keenness of her other senses was ___(e)d by use. It is said that she could ___ who was in a room simply by using her sense of smell.

attest
nocturna   7–8. Anyone who has ever gone to college can ___ to the fact that during final exams, many students become ___ animals. They study all night before an exam and then, once the test is over, sleep the rest of the day.

_____ 9–10. The reason the boss likes to ___ Oliver on lengthy errands is no ___. Everyone knows that the office functions better with Oliver out of the way.

_____

Final Check: *Animal Senses*

Here is a final opportunity for you to strengthen your knowledge of the ten words. First read the following selection carefully. Then fill in each blank with a word from the box at the top of the previous page. (Context clues will help you figure out which word goes in which blank.) Use each word once.

Animals possess sensory powers that humans lack. Homing pigeons fly with great speed and accuracy when (1)_____dispatch_____(e)d with messages to faraway places. How do pigeons (2)_____orient_____ themselves in unfamiliar regions? This remains something of a(n) (3)_____enigma_____. The mystery, however, is partly explained by a pigeon's ability to see ultraviolet light, which reveals the sun's position even through clouds. In addition, pigeons can hear sound waves that have traveled hundreds of miles. These waves (4)_____enhance_____

© vanchai/shutterstock.com

a pigeon's sense of direction by indicating distant mountains and seas. Pigeons even appear to (5)_____discern_____ changes in the earth's magnetic field.

Likewise, bats have impressive (6)_____attribute_____s equally worthy of acclaim°. As (7)_____nocturnal_____ animals, they search for food in complete darkness. They do so by screeching in tones higher than any human can hear and then locating prey by the returning echoes.

Scorpions also (8)_____exemplify_____ the night hunter. Tiny leg hairs enable them to feel vibrations in the sand made by a (9)_____mobile_____ insect as far as two feet away.

People with knowledge of the pigeon, bat, and scorpion can (10)_____attest_____ to the fact that such inventions as the magnetic compass, radar, and the motion detector are nothing new.

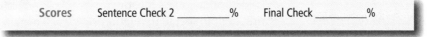

Scores   Sentence Check 2 _____%   Final Check _____%

Enter your scores above and in the **Vocabulary Performance Chart** on the inside back cover of the book.

The box at the right lists twenty-five words from Unit One. Using the clues at the bottom of the page, fill in these words to complete the puzzle that follows.

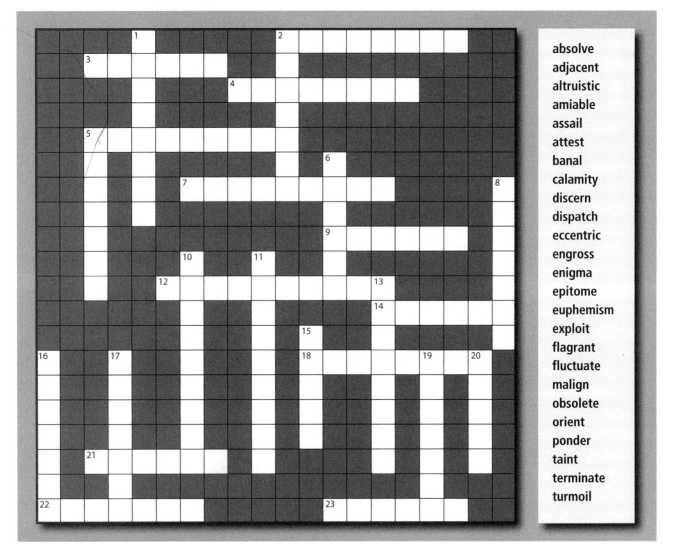

absolve
adjacent
altruistic
amiable
assail
attest
banal
calamity
discern
dispatch
eccentric
engross
enigma
epitome
euphemism
exploit
flagrant
fluctuate
malign
obsolete
orient
ponder
taint
terminate
turmoil

ACROSS

2. To send to a specific place or on specific business

3. To make evil and often untrue statements about; speak evil of

4. No longer active in use; out of date

5. To stop; bring to an end

7. Differing from what is customary; odd *eccentric*

9. A mystery or puzzle *enigma*

12. Unselfishly concerned for the welfare of others; unselfish *altruist*

14. To attack physically or verbally

18. Close; near (to something) *adjacent*

21. To consider carefully; think deeply about

22. A perfect or typical example *epitome*

23. To make a statement about something on the basis of personal experience; bear witness; testify *attest*

DOWN

1. Shockingly obvious; outrageous *flagrant*

2. To recognize; detect *discern*

5. Complete confusion; uproar *turmoil*

6. To determine one's location or direction; to locate in relation to a direction *orient*

8. Good-natured; friendly *amiable*

10. To vary irregularly; to go up and down or back and forth *fluctuate*

11. A mild or vague term used as a substitute for one that is offensive or unpleasant

13. An event bringing great loss or misery *tragedy*

15. Lacking originality; overused; commonplace *banal*

16. To find innocent or blameless *absolve*

17. To use selfishly or unethically; take unfair advantage of *exploit*

19. To hold the full attention of *engross*

20. To stain the honor of someone or something

28

PART A

Choose the word that best completes each item and write it in the space provided.

_____ 1. New York's firefighters and police were the ___ of courage during the attack on the World Trade Center on September 11, 2001. Many of them lost their lives while attempting to save others.

      A. calamity   B. epitome   C. animosity   D. euphemism

_____ 2. The suspect realized that if she wanted to be ___ of the charges, she'd better hire a detective to find the real murderer.

      A. assailed   B. enhanced   C. pondered   D. absolved

_____ 3. According to legend, vampires are ___ creatures who cannot survive in daylight.

      A. altruistic   B. banal   C. nocturnal   D. conventional

_____ 4. The counseling program to ___ addicts includes job training.

      A. rehabilitate   B. attest   C. ponder   D. exemplify

_____ 5. The Peace Corps continues to ___ American volunteers to live and work in developing nations.

      A. discern   B. appease   C. dispatch   D. fluctuate

_____ 6. In a race across New Jersey in 1901, drivers traveling up to thirty miles an hour were arrested for their ___ disregard of the speed limit, which was eight miles an hour.

      A. flagrant   B. altruistic   C. banal   D. conventional

_____ 7. In the winter, the price of tomatoes ___ while their quality goes down.

      A. elicits   B. appeases   C. escalates   D. absolves

_____ 8. A common ___ for _dead body_ is "remains."

      A. acclaim   B. attribute   C. euphemism   D. turmoil

_____ 9. The taxi driver was so ___ that he charged his own mother for a ride.

      A. mercenary   B. arbitrary   C. mobile   D. obsolete

_____ 10. You probably thought that mail delivery by mule was ___, but it still exists in the Grand Canyon.

      A. adamant   B. mercenary   C. tangible   D. obsolete

(Continues on next page)

PART B

On the answer line, write the letter of the choice that best completes each item.

_____ 11. A person who has lost his or her eyesight can become more **mobile** by
    A. learning to read Braille.
    B. becoming depressed and refusing to go out.
    C. learning to get around with a Seeing Eye dog.
    D. listening to the radio.

_____ 12. The nurse **exploited** her elderly patient by
    A. giving him a bath and changing his sheets.   C. complaining to her husband about him.
    B. reading aloud to him every day.   D. tricking him into giving his fortune to her.

_____ 13. The book so **engrossed** Bob that he
    A. complained aloud about how disgusting and distasteful it was.
    B. didn't even hear me come into the room.
    C. couldn't understand it.
    D. didn't finish reading it.

_____ 14. The tennis player's performance **fluctuated** during the tournament. It
    A. was magnificent one day, awful the next, and average the following day.
    B. was consistently excellent.
    C. began well but went steadily downhill all week.
    D. started badly but became better every day.

_____ 15. You would have an **encounter** with an old friend from grade school if you
    A. contacted him by email.   C. forgot about him.
    B. missed him.   D. ran into him at the mall.

_____ 16. **Conventional** business clothing for a man includes
    A. Bermuda shorts and a Hawaiian shirt.   C. a suit and tie.
    B. jeans and a sleeveless tank top.   D. swimming trunks

_____ 17. The office manager **maligned** her boss by saying,
    A. "He's not only stupid but also dishonest."   C. "He's the nicest boss I've ever had."
    B. "I wish I had a sports car like his."   D. "I think he could be a little more efficient."

_____ 18. Our English teacher says spring fever is a **syndrome** that includes
    A. March through June.   C. an urge to stare sleepily out the window.
    B. beautiful daffodils.   D. allergy pills.

_____ 19. "You have **tainted** the name of our family forever," Ellen's father told her, "and you should be
    A. proud."   C. amused."
    B. ashamed."   D. thanked."

_____ 20. In order to **attest** to what it feels like to walk on the moon's surface, a person must
    A. have read about an astronaut who did it.   C. be a scientist who has studied the moon.
    B. have walked there himself or herself.   D. have a good imagination.

Score   (Number correct) _____ x 5 = _____%

PART A

Complete each item with a word from the box. Use each word once.

A. **acclaim**	B. **adamant**	C. **allusion**	D. **antagonist**	E. **appease**
F. **attribute**	G. **comprehensive**	H. **elicit**	I. **enigma**	J. **orient**
K. **persevere**	L. **terminate**	M. **venture**		

_____ 1. To get a bachelor's degree from some universities, students must take a(n) ___ exam that tests their overall knowledge of their major field.

_____ 2. Although Marilyn Monroe received great ___ from adoring fans and critics, she never received an Academy Award.

_____ 3. Our congressional representative, ___ in her opposition to pesticides, often reminds voters that pesticides kill about fourteen thousand people each year.

_____ 4. In 1876, Wild Bill Hickok was in a poker game that was ___(e)d by a bullet entering the back of his head.

_____ 5. "Gina isn't the only athlete in the family," Clarence said, making a(n) ___ to Gina's father, a bowling champion.

_____ 6. The thousands of oak leaves that covered the ground in a Scottish town in 1889 were a(n) ___. The nearest oak trees were eight miles away.

_____ 7. Marathon runners must ___ beyond the point at which they start to feel pain.

_____ 8. The ___s in the debate took opposing sides on the question of outlawing cigarettes.

_____ 9. People who can't read must ___ themselves in a city by relating to familiar places, not signs.

_____ 10. In my dreams, I ___ to perform feats that I would never dare when awake, such as leaping from roof to roof along a row of houses.

_____ 11. In some religions, gods and goddesses represent various human ___s, such as strength, beauty, and wisdom.

_____ 12. Apparently, the chance to be President of the United States doesn't ___ much enthusiasm from most Americans. According to one poll, 89 percent say they wouldn't want the job.

_____ 13. When Kathleen stood Evan up for the prom, an apology did not ___ him. He's suing her for the cost of his rented tux and the prom tickets.

(Continues on next page)

PART B

Write **C** if the italicized word is used **correctly**. Write **I** if the word is used **incorrectly**.

_____ 14. If you worry about the environment, you're *eccentric*. According to a recent poll, two-thirds of Americans are concerned about the environment.

_____ 15. Phyllis is very *methodical* in her efforts to be the life of any party. She keeps a file box of jokes, indexed by occasion.

__C__ 16. We had to trim the oak tree *adjacent* to our house so that its branches wouldn't reach into the porch.

_____ 17. Our *amiable* neighbor scares our children so much that they refuse to knock on his door even on Halloween.

_____ 18. In 1971, three dolphins *assailed* a drowning woman by keeping her afloat and protecting her from sharks across two hundred miles of ocean.

__C__ 19. Lightning bolts, which travel at millions of miles an hour and produce five times the heat of the sun's surface, *exemplify* nature's tremendous energy.

_____ 20. The *turmoil* of a smooth, clear lake always makes me feel at peace.

__C__ 21. A wedding ring is a *tangible* expression of a couple's commitment to each other.

_____ 22. Every day, people *enhance* the tropical rainforests by destroying some twenty thousand acres.

_____ 23. The passerby showed his *animosity* by entering the burning house and pulling the child to safety.

__C__ 24. When the evidence in a case is unclear, a jury's decision may be *arbitrary*, based on only the jurors' "gut feeling."

_____ 25. James Bond was about to step into his enemy's trap when a beautiful woman, a former enemy who had fallen in love with him, *pondered* him to escape.

Score   (Number correct) _____ x 4 = _____%

PART A: Synonyms

In the space provided, write the letter of the choice that is most nearly the **same** in meaning as the **boldfaced** word.

_____ 1. **antagonist**   A. opponent   B. supporter   C. question   D. response

_____ 2. **exploit**   A. assist   B. take advantage of   C. leave   D. increase

_____ 3. **euphemism**   A. quotation   B. main point   C. trait   D. inoffensive term

_____ 4. **orient**   A. consider carefully   B. please   C. continue   D. locate

_____ 5. **appease**   A. end   B. calm down   C. take advantage of   D. begin

_____ 6. **discern**   A. see   B. forget   C. interest   D. deny

_____ 7. **rehabilitate**   A. repeat   B. come upon   C. restore to normality   D. clear of guilt

_____ 8. **attribute**   A. confusion   B. characteristic   C. regret   D. ill will

_____ 9. **venture**   A. dare   B. increase   C. improve   D. intrude on

_____ 10. **epitome**   A. perfect model   B. puzzle   C. goal   D. exception

_____ 11. **syndrome**   A. confusion   B. reference   C. typical symptoms   D. main point

_____ 12. **flagrant**   A. unlikely   B. out of date   C. outrageous   D. true

_____ 13. **dispatch**   A. vary   B. repair   C. show   D. send

_____ 14. **enigma**   A. riddle   B. example   C. term   D. disaster

_____ 15. **tangible**   A. movable   B. spiritual   C. calm   D. touchable

_____ 16. **calamity**   A. invention   B. anger   C. tragedy   D. event

_____ 17. **attest**   A. testify   B. teach   C. respond   D. stain

_____ 18. **elicit**   A. state   B. attack   C. draw out   D. avoid

_____ 19. **allusion**   A. problem   B. reference   C. behavior   D. insult

_____ 20. **fluctuate**   A. lean   B. vary   C. prevent   D. stand still

_____ 21. **encounter**   A. meeting   B. opponent   C. continuation   D. characteristic

_____ 22. **ponder**   A. recognize   B. think over   C. use   D. refuse

_____ 23. **arbitrary**   A. illegal   B. governed by law   C. odd   D. based on impulse

_____ 24. **exemplify**   A. praise   B. excuse   C. illustrate   D. send for

_____ 25. **obsolete**   A. personal   B. old-fashioned   C. noisy   D. commonplace

(Continues on next page)

PART B: Antonyms

In the space provided, write the letter of the choice that is most nearly the **opposite** in meaning to the **boldfaced** word.

_____ 26. **adamant**   A. straightforward   B. greedy   C. enormous   D. flexible

_____ 27. **escalate**   A. lessen   B. lift   C. cause   D. form an opinion

_____ 28. **mercenary**   A. rich   B. unusual   C. generous   D. careless

_____ 29. **terminate**   A. begin   B. study   C. pay attention to   D. compete

_____ 30. **malign**   A. recover   B. praise   C. be consistent   D. move

_____ 31. **turmoil**   A. admiration   B. peace and quiet   C. blessing   D. reality

_____ 32. **amiable**   A. nearby   B. disagreeable   C. athletic   D. unusual

_____ 33. **adjacent**   A. unfamiliar   B. distant   C. ordinary   D. unclear

_____ 34. **methodical**   A. clear   B. late   C. generous   D. disorganized

_____ 35. **taint**   A. honor   B. delay   C. surprise   D. interfere

_____ 36. **conventional**   A. lonely   B. uncommon   C. inconvenient   D. noticeable

_____ 37. **nocturnal**   A. early   B. late   C. normal   D. by day

_____ 38. **altruistic**   A. unfriendly   B. selfish   C. usual   D. not well-known

_____ 39. **comprehensive**   A. interesting   B. puzzling   C. limited   D. obvious

_____ 40. **assail**   A. avoid   B. continue   C. stop   D. defend

_____ 41. **enhance**   A. prove   B. worsen   C. support   D. resist

_____ 42. **acclaim**   A. statement   B. recognition   C. criticism   D. assistance

_____ 43. **banal**   A. original   B. old   C. orderly   D. unselfish

_____ 44. **amoral**   A. dependable   B. calm   C. ethical   D. based on personal choice

_____ 45. **mobile**   A. medical   B. immovable   C. harmful   D. cautious

_____ 46. **absolve**   A. blame   B. solve   C. bring to a state of peace   D. annoy

_____ 47. **eccentric**   A. nearby   B. generous   C. ordinary   D. disorganized

_____ 48. **persevere**   A. build   B. add to   C. blame   D. quit

_____ 49. **animosity**   A. spirituality   B. beauty   C. opposition   D. friendliness

_____ 50. **engross**   A. delight   B. bore   C. make active   D. discourage

Score   (Number correct) _____   x 2 = _____ %

Enter your score above and in the **Vocabulary Performance Chart** on the inside back cover of the book.

Each item below starts with a pair of words in CAPITAL LETTERS. For each item, figure out the relationship between these two words. Then decide which of the choices (A, B, C, or D) expresses a similar relationship. Write the letter of your choice on the answer line.

_____ 1. METHODICAL : ORGANIZED ::
    A. careful : sloppy   C. simple : elaborate
    B. careful : orderly   D. insult : anger

_____ 2. OBSOLETE : TYPEWRITER ::
    A. well-known : Disney World   C. spotlight : flashlight
    B. old-fashioned : modern   D. nutritious : chewing gum

_____ 3. TANGIBLE : DREAMS ::
    A. weather : snowy   C. frequent : often
    B. probable : likely   D. intentional : accident

_____ 4. TERMINATE : EMPLOYMENT ::
    A. chimney : house   C. remember : forget
    B. begin : commence   D. quit : school

_____ 5. ABSOLVE : BLAME ::
    A. reduce : enlarge   C. trial : verdict
    B. blame : punish   D. wish : desire

_____ 6. AMORAL : CRIMINAL ::
    A. pastor : church   C. uneducated : professor
    B. murderer : victim   D. brave : explorer

_____ 7. ANTAGONIST : TEAMMATE ::
    A. coworker : relative   C. scholar : athlete
    B. opponent : supporter   D. teammate : coach

_____ 8. ACCLAIM : CRITIC ::
    A. test : question   C. loyalty : dog
    B. statement : silence   D. symptom : disease

_____ 9. ADJACENT : NEARBY ::
    A. neighboring : distant   C. optimistic : cheerful
    B. familiar : strange   D. optimist : whiner

_____ 10. ENGROSS : FASCINATING ::
    A. popular : well-known   C. boring : thrilling
    B. common : rare   D. bore : monotonous

(Continues on next page)

____ 11. CONVENTIONAL : UNCOMMON ::
     A. conduct : experiment   C. owner : possesses
     B. thoughtful : considerate   D. quiet : noisy

____ 12. MOBILE : UNMOVING ::
     A. rapid : slow   C. excited : lively
     B. write : words   D. wet : water

____ 13. ENIGMA : MYSTERIOUS ::
     A. baseball : bat   C. funny : serious
     B. joke : funny   D. clue : detective

____ 14. OWL : NOCTURNAL ::
     A. tiger : cat   C. day : night
     B. tiger : fierce   D. child : adult

____ 15. DISCERN : LOOK ::
     A. hear : listen   C. cold : touch
     B. smell : taste   D. ignore : see

____ 16. ALTRUISTIC : UNSELFISH ::
     A. saint : holy   C. generous : stingy
     B. artist : painting   D. wealthy : rich

____ 17. BANAL : UNORIGINAL ::
     A. surprising : unexpected   C. copied : original
     B. pleasant : distasteful   D. match : fire

____ 18. CALAMITY : SUFFERING ::
     A. magnet : repels   C. tragedy : sadness
     B. tragedy : joy   D. table : chair

____ 19. PERSEVERE : QUIT ::
     A. open : shut   C. drink : thirsty
     B. perspire : sweat   D. continue : persist

____ 20. VENTURE : EXPLORER ::
     A. see : blind person   C. cow : milk
     B. teach : professor   D. ocean : ship

Score   (Number correct) _____ x 5 = _____%

Enter your score above and in the **Vocabulary Performance Chart** on the inside back cover of the book.

Unit Two

Chapter 6

concurrent	hypothetical
confiscate	nominal
constitute	predominant
decipher	prerequisite
default	recession

Chapter 7

degenerate	sanctuary
implausible	scrutiny
incoherent	sinister
intercede	suffice
intricate	vulnerable

Chapter 8

blatant	gloat
blight	immaculate
contrive	plagiarism
garble	qualm
gaunt	retaliate

Chapter 9

curtail	indispensable
devastate	intermittent
digress	rigor
incentive	squander
incorporate	succumb

Chapter 10

alleviate	infamous
benefactor	intrinsic
covert	revulsion
cynic	speculate
demise	virile

CHAPTER 6

concurrent	hypothetical
confiscate	nominal
constitute	predominant
decipher	prerequisite
default	recession

Ten Words in Context

In the space provided, write the letter of the meaning closest to that of each **boldfaced** word. Use the context of the sentences to help you figure out each word's meaning.

1 concurrent
(kən-kûr′ənt)
-*adjective*

● Having mistakenly registered for two **concurrent** classes, Joe had to drop one of them and choose a course that met at a different time.

● **Concurrent** with the closing of the steel mill was the opening of a new toy factory in town. As a result, most of the workers laid off from the mill found jobs at the new factory.

___ *Concurrent* means   A. occurring at the same time.   B. resulting.   C. noticeable.

2 confiscate
(kŏn′fĭs-kāt′)
-*verb*

● "Hand 'em over," my father said. Just as we were really starting to have fun, he **confiscated** our entire supply of water balloons.

● Los Angeles airport officials recently **confiscated** dozens of wild birds from a man who tried to sneak them into the U.S. inside his suitcase.

___ *Confiscate* means   A. to distribute widely.   B. to take possession of.   C. to overlook.

3 constitute
(kŏn′stĭ-tōōt)
-*verb*

● In my opinion, a good movie, a pizza, and animated conversation **constitute** a perfect night out.

● Twelve business and professional people **constitute** the board of directors of the women's shelter. Among other things, they help raise funds for the shelter.

___ *Constitute* means   A. to repeat.   B. to oppose.   C. to form.

4 decipher
(dĭ-sī′fər)
-*verb*

● Why do contracts have to use language that's so difficult to **decipher**?

● If your teacher can't **decipher** your handwriting, you'll need to write your papers on a computer.

___ *Decipher* means   A. to figure out.   B. to find.   C. to improve.

5 default
(dĭ-fôlt′)
-*verb*

● We won our case against the appliance repairman because he **defaulted** by failing to appear in court.

● Eli's mother said, "I'll co-sign on your car loan, but you have to make every payment. If you **default**, it will hurt my credit rating."

___ *Default* means   A. to act as expected.   B. not to do something required.   C. to begin.

6 hypothetical
(hī′pō-thĕt′ĭ-kəl)
-*adjective*

● Imagine the **hypothetical** situation of going to live alone on an island with no internet. Which books and music would you take along?

● Law schools hold pretend court sessions with **hypothetical** cases so that students can practice their skills.

___ *Hypothetical* means   A. sure to happen.   B. dangerous.   C. imaginary.

7 nominal
(nŏm′ə-nəl)
-adjective

● Except for a **nominal** registration fee, the camp for needy children is entirely free.

● Professor Banks gave us only **nominal** extra credit for participating in psychology experiments. She wanted our course grade to be based mainly on our test scores.

___ *Nominal* means   A. enormous.   B. very little.   C. helpful.

8 predominant
(prĭ-dŏm′ə-nənt)
-adjective

● Rock is the **predominant** music on that radio station, but country music is also played.

● Although the **predominant** type of car in New York City in 1900 used gasoline, a third of the cars ran on electricity.

___ *Predominant* means   A. rare.   B. main.   C. temporary.

9 prerequisite
(prē-rĕk′wĭ-zĭt)
-noun

● You can't take Spanish III unless you've taken the **prerequisite**, Spanish II.

● Since she was allergic to cigarette smoke, Kaylin told Troy that his quitting smoking was a **prerequisite** for their marrying.

___ *Prerequisite* means   A. a requirement.   B. a penalty.   C. a method.

10 recession
(rĭ-sĕsh′ən)
-noun

● While seashore businesses in the North suffer a **recession** in the winter, they do very well from spring to fall.

● The department store laid off twenty workers during the **recession**, but it rehired them when business improved.

___ *Recession* means   A. a rapid growth.   B. a sale.   C. an economic setback.

Matching Words with Definitions

Following are definitions of the ten words. Clearly write or print each word next to its definition. The sentences above and on the previous page will help you decide on the meaning of each word.

1. _constitute_ _____ To make up; be the parts of

2. _default_ _____ To fail to do something required

3. _predominant_ _____ Most common or most noticeable

4. _prerequisite_ _____ Something required beforehand

5. _confiscate_ _____ To seize with authority; legally take possession of

6. _decipher_ _____ To interpret or read (something confusing or hard to make out)

7. _nominal_ _____ Slight; very small compared with what might be expected

8. _concurrent_ _____ Happening or existing at the same time; simultaneous

9. _recession_ _____ A temporary decline in business

10. _hypothetical_ _____ Supposed for the sake of argument or examination; imaginary; theoretical

CAUTION: Do not go any further until you are sure the above answers are correct. Then you can use the definitions to help you in the following practices. Your goal is eventually to know the words well enough so that you don't need to check the definitions at all.

Sentence Check 1

Using the answer line provided, complete each item below with the correct word from the box. Use each word once.

A. concurrent	B. confiscate	C. constitute	D. decipher	E. default
F. hypothetical	G. nominal	H. predominant	I. prerequisite	J. recession

_____ 1. Our local public library charges only a ___ fine for late books but a higher fine for late DVDs.

_____ 2. A ___ for taking the driver's road test is passing a written test on the state's driving laws.

_____constitute_____ 3. One hundred senators and 435 members of the House of Representatives ___ the United States Congress.

_____concurrent_____ 4. Although the two robberies were ___—both occurred at midnight on Friday—one man had planned them both.

_____ 5. Anger was the ___ emotion among voters when they first heard that their taxes would be raised again.

_____ 6. To teach young children safety, many parents explain what to do in ___ situations, such as if a stranger asks them to go for a ride.

_____ 7. After Justine borrowed the family car without permission for the third time, her parents ___(ed) her driver's license.

_____ 8. The wireless phone company refused to open another account in Glen's name because he had ___(e)d on several of his previous bills.

_____ 9. When the shoe factory closed, our little town went into a ___ because the laid-off workers had no money to spend at local businesses.

_____ 10. Karim is such a bad speller that his wife couldn't ___ his text message saying she should meet him at the restaurant.

NOTE: Now check your answers to these items by turning to page 129. Going over the answers carefully will help you prepare for the next two practices, for which answers are not given.

Sentence Check 2

Using the answer lines provided, complete each item below with **two** words from the box. Use each word once.

_____
_____ 1–2. These instructions are in such tiny type, a magnifying glass is a ___ for being able to ___ them.

_____constitute_____
_____predominant_____ 3–4. Although cancer and heart disease ___ the leading threats to life in the United States, car accidents are the ___ cause of death for teenagers.

_____nominal_____
_____ 5–6. This summer, local children can sign up for art or music lessons for a ___ fee of $3. They can't take both, though, since the classes will be ___.

_____concurrent_____

hypothetical
recession

7–8. When Ms. Howe was interviewed for the job of store manager, the regional manager asked her a question about a ___ situation. "Imagine that our business is in a ___," he said. "What would you do to enhance° sales?"

default
confiscate

9–10. The small print on the Bryants' mortgage stated that if they should ___ on payments, the bank had the right to ___ their house.

Final Check: *Money Problems*

Here is a final opportunity for you to strengthen your knowledge of the ten words. First read the following selection carefully. Then fill in each blank with a word from the box at the top of the previous page. (Context clues will help you figure out which word goes in which blank.) Use each word once.

My neighbor, Martha, ran into my house crying and angry. "My car has been stolen!" she gasped. "I saw them take it!"

I called the police for her, and she told an officer the license number and car model. "The (1)_____ color of the car is white," she added, "but it has a black roof. I had it parked in the lot adjacent° to the beauty shop I own. I saw two men tow it away."

"You saw them tow it away?" the officer asked. "Have you (2)_____(e)d on your car loan?"

"What do you mean?" Martha asked.

"If you haven't been making your payments, the bank or dealer has the right to (3)_____ the car."

Martha admitted that she hadn't made any payments for three months. Later she told me she'd gotten notices in the mail but threw them away because their language was too complicated to (4)_____. She also said she was having money problems. (5)_____ with the car loan was a big home-improvement loan. She also had five credit-card bills and regular living expenses to pay. To top it all off, the city was suffering from a (6)_____, so her income was down, something her laid-off employees could certainly attest° to. She was about $12,000 in debt.

At my suggestion, Martha visited a debt counselor, who helped her develop a comprehensive° plan to pay her bills. The only (7)_____s for this free service were a regular job and a willingness to pay one's debts in full. The counselor and Martha planned what would (8)_____ a reasonable budget, based on Martha's income and expenses. They then wrote to the companies she owed to arrange to pay a (9)_____ amount each month until the whole debt was paid. They also discussed what she would do in several (10)_____ situations, such as if her refrigerator died or her income changed.

Now, Martha is getting back on her feet again—in more ways than one, since she never got the car back.

Scores   Sentence Check 2 _____%   Final Check _____%

CHAPTER

7

degenerate	sanctuary
implausible	scrutiny
incoherent	sinister
intercede	suffice
intricate	vulnerable

Ten Words in Context

In the space provided, write the letter of the meaning closest to that of each **boldfaced** word. Use the context of the sentences to help you figure out each word's meaning.

1 degenerate
(dĭ-jĕn′ər-āt′)
-verb

- Mr. Freedman's family was called to the nursing home when the old man's condition began to **degenerate**. It was feared he didn't have long to live.
- Mel's relationship with his parents **degenerated** when he dropped out of school against their wishes and became a bartender.

___ *Degenerate* means   A. to improve.   B. to remain the same.   C. to get worse.

2 implausible
(ĭm-plô′zə-bəl)
-adjective

- As **implausible** as it may sound, southern Florida sometimes does get snow.
- Insurance companies hear such **implausible** excuses for auto accidents as "I hit the telephone pole when I was blinded by the lights of a flying saucer."

___ *Implausible* means   A. unbelievable.   B. acceptable.   C. valuable.

3 incoherent
(ĭn′kō-hîr′ənt)
-adjective

- If Mitch doesn't get some sleep soon, he'll become completely **incoherent**. He's so tired that he's already having trouble expressing his thoughts clearly.
- My sister talks a lot in her sleep, but she's so **incoherent** then that we can never figure out what she's saying.

___ *Incoherent* means   A. calm.   B. unclear.   C. inconvenient.

4 intercede
(ĭn′tər-sēd′)
-verb

- When the principal said Harry couldn't play in Friday's football game, the coach **interceded**, hoping to change the principal's mind.
- Inez's parents refused to come to her wedding until her brother **interceded** and persuaded them to come after all.

___ *Intercede* means   A. to give in to someone.   B. to plead for someone.   C. to examine closely.

5 intricate
(ĭn′trĭ-kĭt)
-adjective

- *War and Peace* is a long, **intricate** novel that weaves together the detailed life stories of many individuals.
- It's amazing to see the **intricate** gold and silver jewelry that ancient Indians made with only simple tools. It obviously required great patience and skill to create such complex ornaments.

___ *Intricate* means   A. simple.   B. uninteresting.   C. complicated.

6 sanctuary
(săngk′chōō-ĕr′ē)
-noun

- Old, unused trains in Grand Central Station serve as a nighttime **sanctuary** for some of New York City's homeless.
- When the houseful of children becomes too noisy, Ned finds the laundry room to be a **sanctuary**, a place where he can read in quiet.

___ *Sanctuary* means   A. a reminder.   B. a shelter.   C. a challenge.

7 scrutiny
(skrōōt′ən-ē)
-noun

● Store security guards give careful **scrutiny** to people carrying large bags, since the bags may be used for shoplifting.

● Before being published, a book comes under the **scrutiny** of a proofreader, who examines it for grammar and spelling errors.

___ *Scrutiny* means   A. attention.   B. protection.   C. permission.

8 sinister
(sĭn′ĭs-tər)
-adjective

● In the movie, a mad scientist thought up the **sinister** scheme of releasing a deadly virus. His evil plot failed when he died from the virus himself.

● The creepy novel *The Boys from Brazil* tells of a **sinister** plot to clone dozens of copies of Adolf Hitler who would then take over the world.

___ *Sinister* means   A. illogical.   B. evil.   C. inconsiderate.

9 suffice
(sə-fīs′)
-verb

● The amount of research you've done may **suffice** for a high-school term paper, but not for a college essay.

● I forgot to buy something for lunch tomorrow, but the leftover meatloaf will **suffice**.

___ *Suffice* means   A. to be wasted.   B. to be adequate.   C. to be examined.

10 vulnerable
(vŭl′nər-ə-bəl)
-adjective

● Homes in heavily wooded areas are especially **vulnerable** to termites.

● Because of rising ocean levels, many coastal communities are **vulnerable** to flooding.

___ *Vulnerable* means   A. open.   B. safe.   C. attracted.

Matching Words with Definitions

Following are definitions of the ten words. Clearly write or print each word next to its definition. The sentences above and on the previous page will help you decide on the meaning of each word.

1. _____ Having many parts arranged in a complicated way; complex

2. _____ To be good enough

3. _____ To worsen; deteriorate

4. _____ A place of safety, protection, or relief

5. _____ To make a request or plead on behalf of someone else

6. _____ Open to damage or attack; susceptible

7. _____ Difficult to believe; unlikely

8. _____ Evil; wicked

9. _____ Close inspection; careful examination

10. _____ Unable to speak in an orderly, logical way

CAUTION: Do not go any further until you are sure the above answers are correct. Then you can use the definitions to help you in the following practices. Your goal is eventually to know the words well enough so that you don't need to check the definitions at all.

Sentence Check 1

Using the answer line provided, complete each item below with the correct word from the box. Use each word once.

A. degenerate	B. implausible	C. incoherent	D. intercede	E. intricate
F. sanctuary	G. scrutiny	H. sinister	I. suffice	J. vulnerable

_____ 1. Although it seems ___, the seemingly dead desert really does blossom after a rainstorm.

_____ 2. The leaves outside the window created a(n) ___, lacy shadow on my bedroom wall.

_____ 3. People who live in big cities are more ___ to muggings than are residents of small towns.

_____ 4. In the *Batman* movies, the Joker's name is misleading, for he's a(n) ___ man who takes pleasure in doing evil.

_____ 5. Ken's cartoons ___ for the school newspaper, but they wouldn't be good enough for the city papers.

_____ 6. When Dad informed my little sister that she had to be home from her date no later than ten o'clock, Mom ___(e)d and gave her a midnight curfew.

_____ 7. When I don't have company, my apartment tends to ___ into a jumble of papers, clothes, and school supplies.

_____ 8. Unclaimed bags at airports receive the ___ of security officers watching for drugs or explosives.

_____ 9. My brother was so upset that he was ___. It wasn't until he calmed down that I understood what he was saying: that he had been fired.

_____ 10. People who allow an escaped convict to use their home as a ___ may face criminal charges themselves.

NOTE: Now check your answers to these items by turning to page 129. Going over the answers carefully will help you prepare for the next two practices, for which answers are not given.

Sentence Check 2

Using the answer lines provided, complete each item below with **two** words from the box. Use each word once.

~~intricate~~
~~degenerate~~

1–2. When a complicated musical piece is played by a talented orchestra, audiences can appreciate the ___ structure. But when poor musicians try the piece, it usually ___s into noise.

~~implausible~~
_____

3–4. To get into the party, Malcolm made up a flagrant° lie—a(n) ___ story about having lost our invitations in a fire. However, the unlikely tale did not ___ to get us in.

~~vulnerable~~
~~sanctuary~~

5–6. Birds feel ___ to attack when they are out in the open where shrubbery is sparse. To attract them to your bird feeder, put it near a ___ of thickly growing trees and large bushes.

scrutiny

intercede

    7–8. The children's eager ___ of the carefully arranged candies and cookies brought a warning from their mother: "Look, but don't touch!" However, their grandmother ___(e)d and convinced her that it would be unjust to give all the goodies to company and none to the children.

sinister

    9–10. As he left the bank, the robber shot and wounded an elderly man on mere impulse. Shocked by the ___ act, the bank clerk was at first ___. However, after calming down, she was able to clearly tell the police about the robbery and the totally arbitrary° shooting.

Final Check: *The New French Employee*

Here is a final opportunity for you to strengthen your knowledge of the ten words. First read the following selection carefully. Then fill in each blank with a word from the box at the top of the previous page. (Context clues will help you figure out which word goes in which blank.) Use each word once.

© tennis/shutterstock.com

    One summer, Nan worked in a factory with an employee who had recently arrived from France, a soft-spoken young man named Jean-Louis. He spoke little English, but Nan's basic French (1)_____(e)d for simple conversations and helpful translations.

    However, one day when she was called to the foreman's office, she wished she knew no French at all. FBI agents were there with Jean-Louis. After explaining that Jean-Louis may have been more (2)_____ than the innocent young man he appeared to be, the foreman left her there to translate for the agents. The agents said Jean-Louis had been on the run after committing several jewel thefts in France. They had already been to Jean-Louis's apartment and confiscated° a diamond necklace and some expensive watches. Nan struggled to translate their questions, which were often too (3)_____ for her limited vocabulary. At times, she became so nervous that she was nearly (4)_____. When Jean-Louis finally deciphered° what Nan was saying, he said the police were maligning° him. He claimed he was being mistaken for his no-good twin brother, who was responsible for the robberies, and therefore he was innocent—he should be absolved° of all blame. The angry FBI agents found Jean-Louis's story (5)_____. The conversation soon (6)_____(e)d into a shouting match, with everyone yelling at poor Nan. When her boss heard the racket, he (7)_____(e)d, appeased° the agents, and got them to excuse her.

    Nan then went to the ladies' room, a (8)_____ from the turmoil° of all the shouting. After the agents left with Jean-Louis, she was calm enough to go back to work. But she felt (9)_____ for days as she wondered if she was under the (10)_____ of jewel thieves who might blame her for Jean-Louis's arrest.

Scores　　Sentence Check 2 _____%　　Final Check _____%

CHAPTER

8

blatant	gloat
blight	immaculate
contrive	plagiarism
garble	qualm
gaunt	retaliate

Ten Words in Context

In the space provided, write the letter of the meaning closest to that of each **boldfaced** word. Use the context of the sentences to help you figure out each word's meaning.

1 blatant
(blā′tənt)
-*adjective*

● Eva is a **blatant** bargain-hunter. Not only does she wait for end-of season sales, but she chooses an already-reduced item and then asks if the salesperson will accept a lower price.

● The company's disregard of the environment is **blatant**. It makes no effort to stop polluting coastal waters with garbage.

__ *Blatant* means A. unmistakable.   B. scrambled.   C. not noticeable.

2 blight
(blīt)
-*noun*

● Nothing has hurt our country more than the **blight** of drug addiction.

● There are two ways of looking at TV: as a valuable source of information or as a **blight** that dulls the mind.

__ *Blight* means A. something that assists.   B. something that is new.   C. something that harms.

3 contrive
(kən-trīv′)
-*verb*

● My eight-year-old son could write a book titled *101 Ways I Have **Contrived** to Stay Up Past My Bedtime.*

● Jill has to **contrive** a way to get a day off from work for her friend's wedding. She's already used up her vacation time.

__ *Contrive* means A. to think up.   B. to mix up.   C. to avoid.

4 garble
(gär′bəl)
-*verb*

● The new reporter **garbled** the newspaper story; the result was an article that made no sense at all.

● The company had **garbled** the bike's assembly instructions so badly that we were constantly confused about which step to do next.

__ *Garble* means A. to read.   B. to lose.   C. to jumble.

5 gaunt
(gônt)
-*adjective*

● Abraham Lincoln's beard made his **gaunt** face look fuller.

● Sharon's eating disorder, called anorexia nervosa, has made her so **gaunt** that she looks like a walking skeleton.

__ *Gaunt* means A. very thin.   B. wide.   C. confused.

6 gloat
(glōt)
-*verb*

● The coach told his team, "There's only one thing worse than a sore loser, and that's a mean winner. Don't **gloat**."

● Neil's sister always tattles on him and then **gloats** when he's punished, saying, "I told you so."

__ *Gloat* means A. to apologize fully.   B. to be overly self-satisfied.   C. to pay back.

46

7 immaculate
(ĭ-măk′yə-lĭt)
-adjective

- It's amazing that while Carolyn's appearance is always **immaculate**, her apartment often seems very dirty.
- Don't expect a child to come home from a birthday party with **immaculate** clothing. Children often manage to get as much birthday cake on their clothing as in their mouths.

__ *Immaculate* means   A. uncomfortable.   B. spotless.   C. soiled.

8 plagiarism
(plā′jĕ-rĭz′əm)
-noun

- When the author saw a movie with the same plot as one of her novels, she sued for **plagiarism**.
- The teacher warned her students that using an author's exact words as one's own is **plagiarism**.

__ *Plagiarism* means   A. creativity.   B. the stealing of ideas.   C. planning.

9 qualm
(kwôm)
-noun

- Lorenzo is so honest that he has **qualms** about telling "little white lies." For instance, it bothers him to say he likes a friend's new haircut when he really doesn't.
- After hiding Kwan's bike as an April Fool's joke, I began to have **qualms**. What if she thought it was stolen and called the police?

__ *Qualm* means   A. a guilty feeling.   B. a proud memory.   C. a clever plan.

10 retaliate
(rĭ-tăl′ē-āt′)
-verb

- When one toddler snatched away the other's toy, the second child **retaliated** by hitting her with a plastic block.
- When Ron refused to pay his younger brother for washing his car, he **retaliated** by washing it again—with its windows open.

__ *Retaliate* means   A. to forgive.   B. to take revenge.   C. to confuse.

Matching Words with Definitions

Following are definitions of the ten words. Clearly write or print each word next to its definition. The sentences above and on the previous page will help you decide on the meaning of each word.

1. _____ An uneasy feeling about how right or proper a particular action is
2. __blatant__ To mix up or confuse (as a story or message); scramble
3. __gloat__ To feel or express delight or self-satisfaction, often spitefully
4. __blight__ Something that weakens, damages, or destroys
5. __plagiarism__ Using someone else's writings or ideas as one's own
6. _____ To plan cleverly; think up
7. __retaliate__ To return an injury for an injury; pay back
8. _____ Very obvious, often offensively so
9. __immaculate__ Perfectly clean
10. __gaunt__ Thin and bony

CAUTION: Do not go any further until you are sure the above answers are correct. Then you can use the definitions to help you in the following practices. Your goal is eventually to know the words well enough so that you don't need to check the definitions at all.

Sentence Check 1

Using the answer line provided, complete each item below with the correct word from the box. Use each word once.

A. blatant	B. blight	C. contrive	D. garble	E. gaunt
F. gloat	G. immaculate	H. plagiarism	I. qualm	J. retaliate

contrive   1. Emilio still hopes to ___ a way to get Rita to go out with him, even though she's refused him four times.

_____   2. The F's and D's on my brother's report card are ___ evidence of how little he has studied this term.

gloat   3. My aunt refuses to drive Mr. Elson to bingo because he ___s so much when he wins, which is often.

blatant   4. Child abuse is a ___ on the physical and mental health of our youth.

_____   5. A(n) ___ house may be a sign that someone has nothing better to do than clean.

_____   6. Mark Twain joked that charges of ___ were ridiculous because no one can be completely original. He wrote, "We mortals can't create—we can only copy."

_____   7. My parents say it is foolish to give spare change to panhandlers, but I always feel a ___ when I walk by them and give nothing.

_____   8. Rescued after being lost at sea for nine days, the men were terribly ___, but they put on weight rapidly.

_____   9. Every time the Hatfields harmed the McCoys, the McCoys would ___, so the feud went on for years.

_____   10. When my friend Jamee left a message with my little brother, inviting me to go to the mall, my brother ___(e)d it so badly that the message I got was "Jamee wants you to go play ball."

NOTE: Now check your answers to these items by turning to page 129. Going over the answers carefully will help you prepare for the next two practices, for which answers are not given.

Sentence Check 2

Using the answer lines provided, complete each item below with **two** words from the box. Use each word once.

gaunt   1–2. The little girl was so ___ after her illness that her parents carefully ___(e)d
contrive   fattening meals that were sure to arouse her appetite.

retaliate   3–4. After the bully struck him, Jules wanted to ___ by throwing a rock, but he
qualm   had ___s about doing anything so dangerous.

_____   5–6. The living room looked ___ except for a lump under the carpet, a(n) ___ sign
_____   that my son had taken a shortcut in cleaning up.

_____   7–8. Willie is a ___ on our school. Not only does he start fights with opposing
_____   players on the basketball court, but he also ___s after he's benched, as if
                                  he's proud of causing such turmoil°. In fact, although he's a great player, the
                                  coach is pondering° kicking him off the team.

_____   9–10. "At least I know you aren't guilty of ___," said my teacher. "Nobody else
_____   would have ___(e)d the report so badly that it's impossible to follow."

Final Check: _A Cruel Teacher_

Here is a final opportunity for you to strengthen your knowledge of the ten words. First read the following
selection carefully. Then fill in each blank with a word from the box at the top of the previous page.
(Context clues will help you figure out which word goes in which blank.) Use each word once.

It has been twenty years since I was in Mr. Brill's
tenth-grade biology class, but I still get nervous thinking
about it. Mr. Brill was a tall, (1)_____ man
who resembled the skeleton at the back of the room.
His meanness was (2)_____. For his
most difficult questions, he would call on the shyest kids,
those most vulnerable° to the pain of embarrassment. And
when they nervously (3)_____(e)d

their answers, he would (4)_____, as if their poor performance were a
personal victory for him. The discomfort of some of his victims was almost tangible°, nearly as
solid as the wooden pointer which he sometimes loudly slammed across his desk just to shock
us. He seemed to (5)_____ situations just to make us miserable. For example, if
our fingernails were not (6)_____, we were sent out of class. As if we needed
clean hands to dissect a frog! One time I worked extremely hard on a paper for class, but he accused me of
(7)_____. He said I must have copied it because I was too dumb to write anything
that good. Without a (8)_____, he gave me an F, which ruined my average and
discouraged me for the rest of the year. All of us students would imagine ways to get even with him,
but we were too afraid to (9)_____. Why a teacher like that was allowed to
continue teaching was an enigma° to us, one I still have not figured out. In all the years since, I've never met
a person who was such a (10)_____ on the teaching profession.

| Scores | Sentence Check 2 _____% | Final Check _____% |

curtail	indispensable
devastate	intermittent
digress	rigor
incentive	squander
incorporate	succumb

Ten Words in Context

In the space provided, write the letter of the meaning closest to that of each **boldfaced** word. Use the context of the sentences to help you figure out each word's meaning.

1 curtail
(kər-tāl′)
-verb

● Upon hearing reports of a huge snowstorm, the principal **curtailed** the school day so students could go home early.

● I need to **curtail** my volunteer activities so that I can spend more time earning money to pay back a loan.

__ *Curtail* means   A. to combine.   B. to shorten.   C. to extend.

2 devastate
(dĕv′əs-tāt′)
-verb

● News that the bicycle factory is closing **devastated** residents of the small town, especially those who learned they'd be losing their jobs.

● Vera is so fond of Andy. She'll be **devastated** to hear he has cancer.

__ *Devastate* means   A. to thrill.   B. to annoy.   C. to upset greatly.

3 digress
(dī-grĕs′)
-verb

● Professor Rubin never **digresses** during a lecture. Even his jokes relate to the day's topic.

● I tried to teach my three-year-old niece our phone number, but we **digressed** to a discussion of whether Big Bird has an iPad.

__ *Digress* means   A. to listen carefully.   B. to go off the subject.   C. to get up.

4 incentive
(ĭn-sĕn′tĭv)
-noun

● The insurance company offers an **incentive**—a free vacation—to encourage its representatives to make more sales.

● The thought of myself in a bathing suit next summer provides me with an adequate **incentive** to exercise.

__ *Incentive* means   A. encouragement.   B. liberty.   C. change.

5 incorporate
(ĭn-kôr′pər-āt′)
-verb

● Jerry **incorporated** all of his favorite desserts into one: a chocolate-covered banana-cream pecan pie.

● Since the number of young children has gone down in my neighborhood, the two elementary schools have been **incorporated** into one.

__ *Incorporate* means   A. to give up.   B. to join together.   C. to raise.

6 indispensable
(ĭn-dĭ-spĕn′sə-bəl)
-adjective

● Because there's no bus or train service nearby, a car is **indispensable** in my neighborhood.

● When you're broke, you find that many things you thought were **indispensable** aren't actually necessary after all.

__ *Indispensable* means   A. free.   B. needed.   C. expensive.

7 intermittent
(ĭn′tər-mĭt′ənt)
-adjective

- You have to work steadily with your dog to train him well. **Intermittent** practice won't work.
- Dora realized that her weight loss on a diet would be **intermittent**, so she didn't give up when the losses stopped. She knew they would start again.

___ *Intermittent* means   A. irregular.   B. too much.   C. steady.

8 rigor
(rĭg′ər)
-noun

- New Marines must go through the **rigors** of boot camp, such as completing an obstacle course and running several miles a day.
- The **rigor** of working at two part-time jobs while going to school proved too much for Jamal. Exhausted, he quit both jobs.

___ *Rigor* means   A. a gamble.   B. an expense.   C. a hardship.

9 squander
(skwŏn′dər)
-verb

- It's sad to see such a wonderful artist **squander** her talent designing labels for baked-bean cans.
- The company lunchroom now closes promptly at one o'clock so that workers can't **squander** time on long lunch breaks.

___ *Squander* means   A. to share.   B. to misuse.   C. to upset.

10 succumb
(sə-kŭm′)
-verb

- Leah **succumbed** to her daughter's begging and bought her a pet lizard for her birthday.
- Once the suspect was arrested, he quickly **succumbed** and confessed to stealing the car stereo.

___ *Succumb* means   A. to yield.   B. to delay.   C. to anger.

Matching Words with Definitions

Following are definitions of the ten words. Clearly write or print each word next to its definition. The sentences above and on the previous page will help you decide on the meaning of each word.

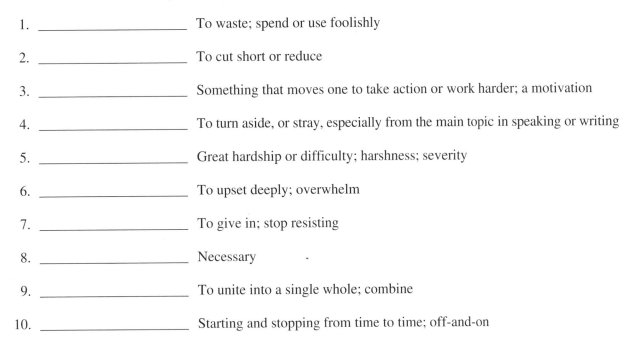

1. _____ To waste; spend or use foolishly

2. _____ To cut short or reduce

3. _____ Something that moves one to take action or work harder; a motivation

4. _____ To turn aside, or stray, especially from the main topic in speaking or writing

5. _____ Great hardship or difficulty; harshness; severity

6. _____ To upset deeply; overwhelm

7. _____ To give in; stop resisting

8. _____ Necessary

9. _____ To unite into a single whole; combine

10. _____ Starting and stopping from time to time; off-and-on

CAUTION: Do not go any further until you are sure the above answers are correct. Then you can use the definitions to help you in the following practices. Your goal is eventually to know the words well enough so that you don't need to check the definitions at all.

Sentence Check 1

Using the answer line provided, complete each item below with the correct word from the box. Use each word once.

A. curtail	B. devastate	C. digress	D. incentive	E. incorporate
F. indispensable	G. intermittent	H. rigor	I. squander	J. succumb

_____ 1. Airlines offer "frequent flier miles" toward free trips as a(n) ___ to get people to fly often.

_____ 2. A computer, a smartphone, and a printer are ___ tools for many self-employed people.

_____ 3. Someone has managed to ___ a tomato and a potato into one plant.

_____ 4. The sight of her bandaged husband in an oxygen tent ___(e)d Claire.

_____ 5. ___ rain kept interrupting the ballgame.

_____ 6. Carl tried hard to ignore the double-fudge chocolate cake on the menu, but he finally ___(e)d and ordered a slice.

_____ 7. Because our history teacher loved to talk, we often could get him to ___ from the lesson by asking him a question about sports or politics.

_____ 8. The man on the street corner offered to sell me a watch, but he quickly ___(e)d his sales pitch when he saw a police officer approaching.

_____ 9. By examining her last two months of spending, Coretta discovered that she had ___(e)d money on too many expensive meals.

_____ 10. Many teenagers don't foresee the ___s of parenthood, such as staying up all night with a sick child.

NOTE: Now check your answers to these items by turning to page 130. Going over the answers carefully will help you prepare for the next two practices, for which answers are not given.

Sentence Check 2

Using the answer lines provided, complete each item below with **two** words from the box. Use each word once.

_____
_____ 1–2. My aunt has only ___ success in quitting smoking. Every few months she ___s to temptation, and then she has to quit all over again.

_____
_____ 3–4. The company decided to ___ the construction of its new plant until the architects could decide on how to ___ an employee gym into the new building.

_____
_____ 5–6. Duane feels he ___(e)d too many years in inactivity, so now he welcomes the ___s of an exercise program.

_____
_____   7–8. The infomercial offered free samples, ninety-day trials, and every other ___ possible to get me to buy the "miracle medicine that would change my life." However, I found the sales pitch highly implausible°. I simply could not believe that this product was ___ to my well-being.

_____resumb_____
_____iro_____   9–10. As Leo explained a failed business deal that had once ___(e)d him, he ___(e)d into the even more interesting tale of his romance with Molly, his business partner.

Final Check: *Learning to Study*

Here is a final opportunity for you to strengthen your knowledge of the ten words. First read the following selection carefully. Then fill in each blank with a word from the box at the top of the previous page. (Context clues will help you figure out which word goes in which blank.) Use each word once.

Linda never had to work very hard to make good grades in high school. But in college, where the (1)_____Rigon_____s of course work were greater, she soon learned that her casual high-school study habits would no longer suffice°. Linda was also learning how easy it was to (2)_____squcolon_____ time online or at parties. She didn't realize how badly she was doing until she saw her midterm grades, which (3)_____aoucaslor_____(e)d her. She knew she had to make some changes right away and began to ponder° what they should be. As a(n) (4)_____incutu_____ to work harder, she tried studying with her friend Denise. But that didn't work; their conversation would (5)_____digress_____ from European history to personal topics, such as dates or favorite songs.

© sirtravelalot/shutterstock.com

Linda decided she'd have to go it alone. She began to skip parties during the week and also to (6)_____holsrescbe_____ the hours she spent on social media. She discovered that a good place to study was (7)_____surcmb_____ to her new study habits. She found the library's silent third floor a sanctuary°, a place with no temptations to which she could (8)_____lncorporcte_____. She also became more methodical° in her study habits, keeping an assignment book, writing due dates on a calendar, and setting up a study schedule. At first, Linda's performance fluctuated°, and so the improvement in her grades was (9)_____—A's and B's alternated with C's and D's. But little by little, she learned to (10)_____ a social life with serious study and earn grades she was proud of.

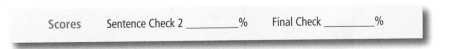
Scores   Sentence Check 2 _____%   Final Check _____%

alleviate	infamous
benefactor	intrinsic
covert	revulsion
cynic	speculate
demise	virile

Ten Words in Context

In the space provided, write the letter of the meaning closest to that of each **boldfaced** word. Use the context of the sentences to help you figure out each word's meaning.

1 alleviate
(ə-lē′vē-āt′)
-verb

- To **alleviate** his loneliness, the widower moved closer to his daughter and her family.
- After a long game in the August heat, the young baseball players **alleviated** their thirst with ice-cold lemonade.

___ *Alleviate* means   A. to consider.   B. to hide.   C. to ease.

2 benefactor
(běn′ə-fǎk′tər)
-noun

- The Second Street Bank is a long-time **benefactor** of the arts. This year it will sponsor a series of free jazz concerts in the park.
- The wealthy **benefactor** who paid for the child's operation prefers to remain anonymous.

___ *Benefactor* means   A. a financial supporter.   B. a social critic.   C. a cooperative person.

3 covert
(kŭv′ərt, kōv′ərt)
-adjective

- Sammy thought his hiding place behind the curtains was **covert**, but his mother could see his toes sticking out.
- If you enjoy **covert** activities, you should become a secret agent.

___ *Covert* means   A. obvious.   B. concealed.   C. easy to bear.

4 cynic
(sĭn′ĭk)
-noun

- Her parents' nasty divorce has made Libby a **cynic** about marriage.
- Mr. Bryant was a **cynic** about people until he fell down on a street corner and several strangers rushed to his aid.

___ *Cynic* means   A. someone who believes the worst.   B. someone who gives help.   C. someone with a bad reputation.

5 demise
(dĭ-mīz′)
-noun

- Everyone in the movie theater cheered when the wicked villain met his **demise** at the hands of Wonder Woman.
- In 1567, a beard caused a man's **demise**. Hans Steininger's beard was so long that he stepped on it while climbing stairs, lost his balance, fell down the steps, and died.

___ *Demise* means   A. popularity.   B. a secret.   C. dying.

6 infamous
(ĭn′fə-məs)
-adjective

- King Henry VIII of England was **infamous** throughout Europe for executing two of his six wives.
- Death Valley, in California, is **infamous** for its extreme temperatures and sudden floods that have killed many travelers.

___ *Infamous* means   A. known unfavorably.   B. thought to be annoying.   C. giving hope.

7 intrinsic
(ĭn-trĭn′sĭk)
-adjective

● Trust is **intrinsic** to any good friendship.
● Because Lian has an **intrinsic** desire to learn, she doesn't need the reward of good grades to motivate her studies.

___ *Intrinsic* means   A. secret.   B. fundamental.   C. unnecessary.

8 revulsion
(rĭ-vŭl′shən)
-noun

● Whenever I read about animal abuse in the newspaper, I am filled with such **revulsion** that I often cannot finish the article.
● When Sharon met the man who had cheated her father out of his life savings, she was overcome with **revulsion**.

___ *Revulsion* means   A. interest.   B. hatred.   C. understanding.

9 speculate
(spĕk′yə-lāt′)
-verb

● It's interesting to **speculate** how history might have been different if Abraham Lincoln had lived a few years longer.
● The therapist asked Cassie to **speculate** about what might happen if she told Leon her true feelings.

___ *Speculate* means   A. to remember.   B. to announce.   C. to guess.

10 virile
(vîr′əl)
-adjective

● Men who are unsure about their masculinity sometimes try to "prove" they are **virile** by being overly aggressive.
● When a male heron stamps his feet and sticks his neck out, and then drops his head and says "plop-buzz," the female finds him very **virile**. In fact, that behavior is how the male attracts a mate.

___ *Virile* means   A. having attractive male qualities.   B. lacking in confidence.   C. unselfish.

Matching Words with Definitions

Following are definitions of the ten words. Clearly write or print each word next to its definition. The sentences above and on the previous page will help you decide on the meaning of each word.

1. _____ Secret; hidden

2. _____ A person who believes the worst of people's behavior and motives; someone who believes people are motivated only by selfishness

3. _____ Belonging to a person or thing by its very nature (and thus not dependent on circumstances); built-in

4. _____ Having a very bad reputation; widely known for being vicious, criminal, or deserving of contempt

5. _____ A person or organization that gives help, especially financial aid

6. _____ Manly; masculine

7. _____ Death

8. _____ To come up with ideas or theories about a subject; theorize

9. _____ To relieve; make easier to endure

10. _____ Great disgust or distaste

CAUTION: Do not go any further until you are sure the above answers are correct. Then you can use the definitions to help you in the following practices. Your goal is eventually to know the words well enough so that you don't need to check the definitions at all.

Sentence Check 1

Using the answer line provided, complete each item below with the correct word from the box. Use each word once.

A. **alleviate**	B. **benefactor**	C. **covert**	D. **cynic**	E. **demise**
F. **infamous**	G. **intrinsic**	H. **revulsion**	I. **speculate**	J. **virile**

_____ 1. Now a popular tourist site, Alcatraz Prison was once ___ for housing some of the most violent and dangerous prisoners in the U.S.

_____ 2. The selfless work of the nuns in the slums of India is enough to touch the hearts of most hardened ___s.

_____ 3. Teenage guys usually welcome a deepening voice and a thickening beard as signs that they are becoming more ___.

_____ 4. My hunger isn't fully satisfied, but the apple ___(e)d it somewhat.

_____ 5. Problems are ___ to life; they're unavoidable.

_____ 6. It's a good idea for married couples to discuss their funeral plans in case of each other's ___. For example, do they wish to be buried or cremated?

_____ 7. Roger Novak had been a well-known ___ of AIDS research, so it was no surprise that he left a lot of money for the research in his will.

_____ 8. "As no group has claimed responsibility, we can only ___ on the motives for the bombing," said the newscaster.

_____ 9. The mere thought of eating meat fills some vegetarians with ___.

_____ 10. The children loved the ___ activities involved in preparing their mother's surprise party.

NOTE: Now check your answers to these items by turning to page 130. Going over the answers carefully will help you prepare for the next two practices, for which answers are not given.

Sentence Check 2

Using the answer lines provided, complete each item below with **two** words from the box. Use each word once.

revulsion
intrustic

1–2. Although everything about the Nazis filled the Dutch spy with ___, his ___ assignment was to make friends with top Nazi scientists. He had few qualms° about faking such friendships—he would have felt more guilty if he hadn't done everything in his power to fight the Nazis.

intrste
allavicke

3–4. Nursing is a good career for Dee because it's a(n) ___ part of her personality to try to ___ people's pain. In addition, her physical and mental strength will help her handle the rigors° of nursing, such as intense stress and long hours.

unfamous

specalte 5–6. With all the stories told about Jesse James, the Dalton Gang, and other ___ figures of the Wild West, we can only ___ as to how much is fact and how much is fiction.

comicunne

benefactor 7–8. Young men who are bullies usually think of themselves as ___, but a ___ of the weak is far more manly than someone who takes advantage of weakness.

_____ 9–10. The ___s in town said that Joyce's sorrow over her husband's ___ was much less than her joy in getting the money from his insurance policy.

demise

Final Check: *The Mad Monk*

Here is a final opportunity for you to strengthen your knowledge of the ten words. First read the following selection carefully. Then fill in each blank with a word from the box at the top of the previous page. (Context clues will help you figure out which word goes in which blank.) Use each word once.

Shortly before the Russian Revolution, an eccentric° man named Rasputin became (1) _infamous_ as the "mad monk." Because he dressed like a peasant, drank heavily, and rarely bathed, the nobility often felt (2) _revulsion_ during their encounters° with him at the palace.

© Courtesy Imperial War Museum.

Yet despite his outward appearance, Rasputin possessed a(n) (3) _intrinsic_ charm that drew many to him, including the Russian empress. She thought him a great man of God and a special (4) _benefactor_ of her seriously ill son, whose condition she felt Rasputin (5) _alleviate_ (e)d.

Many (6) _cynic_ s believed otherwise. To them, Rasputin was no healer; instead, he was a man who exploited° his relationship with the empress for his own benefit. Rather than praise Rasputin, his enemies preferred to malign° him. In a pamphlet titled *The Holy Devil*, one of his critics described him as a sinister° man. This author even dared to (7) _insinuate_ that the monk and the empress were romantically involved. This theory was strengthened by the fact that the empress's "holy man" pursued many women and boasted about how (8) _virile_ he was.

Finally, a group of Russian noblemen made (9) _covert_ plans to kill Rasputin. Somehow, the secret must have gotten out, for a Russian official warned Rasputin of a plot against him. He nevertheless accepted the noblemen's invitation to a dinner party, where they served him poisoned wine and cake. When Rasputin did not appear to succumb° to the poison, his enemies hastened his (10) _demise_ by shooting and stabbing him and then dumping him into an icy river. An autopsy revealed that he had died by drowning.

Scores   Sentence Check 2 _____%   Final Check _____%

Enter your scores above and in the **Vocabulary Performance Chart** on the inside back cover of the book.

The box at the right lists twenty-five words from Unit Two. Using the clues at the bottom of the page, fill in these words to complete the puzzle that follows.

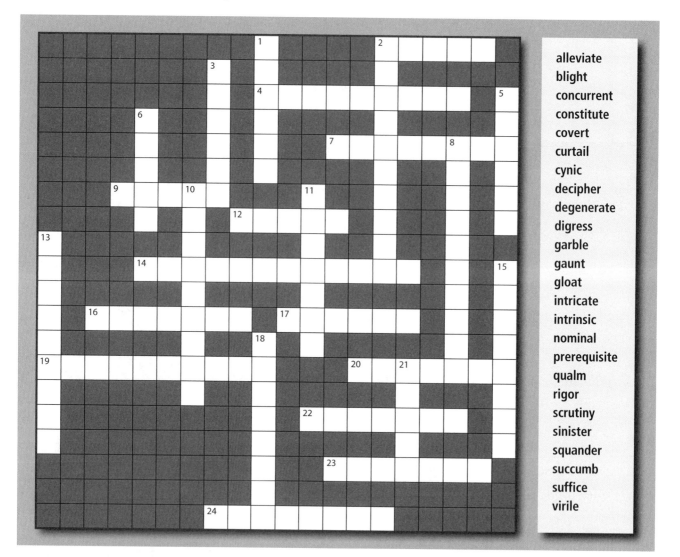

alleviate
blight
concurrent
constitute
covert
curtail
cynic
decipher
degenerate
digress
garble
gaunt
gloat
intricate
intrinsic
nominal
prerequisite
qualm
rigor
scrutiny
sinister
squander
succumb
suffice
virile

ACROSS

2. A person who believes the worst of people's behavior and motives

4. Belonging to a person or thing by its very nature (and thus not dependent on circumstances)

7. To waste; spend or use foolishly

9. To feel or express delight or self-satisfaction, often spitefully

12. Great hardship or difficulty; harshness; severity

14. Something required beforehand

16. To be good enough

17. To mix up or confuse (as a story or message); scramble

19. To make up; be the parts of

20. To turn aside, or stray, especially from the main topic in speaking or writing

22. To give in; stop resisting

23. To cut short or reduce

24. Close inspection; careful examination

DOWN

1. Something that weakens, damages, or destroys

2. Happening or existing at the same time; simultaneous

3. Secret; hidden

5. Manly; masculine

6. An uneasy feeling about how right or proper a particular action is

8. To worsen; deteriorate

10. To relieve; make easier to endure

11. Slight; very small compared with what might be expected

13. Having parts arranged in a complicated way; complex

15. Evil; wicked

18. To interpret or read (something confusing or hard to make out)

21. Thin and bony

PART A

Choose the word that best completes each item and write it in the space provided.

_____ 1. Measles remains a serious ___ worldwide, killing more than 100,000 people each year.

      A. blight   B. plagiarism   C. qualm   D. prerequisite

_____ 2. The nation's student loan program is in serious trouble because many students ___ on their payments.

      A. suffice   B. alleviate   C. intercede   D. default

_____ 3. The CIA's ___ activities often include "bugging" people's homes lines with tiny hidden microphones.

      A. covert   B. blatant   C. virile   D. immaculate

_____ 4. Scientists ___ that the average life span of a dinosaur was probably 100 to 120 years.

      A. speculate   B. digress   C. curtail   D. squander

_____ 5. The ___ of a Connecticut man was strange indeed. He died when his five-hundred-pound wife sat on him.

      A. sanctuary   B. benefactor   C. blight   D. demise

_____ 6. Unless figure skaters practice regularly, their skills will ___.

      A. retaliate   B. degenerate   C. confiscate   D. decipher

_____ 7. It may sound ___, but a camel can drink twenty-five gallons of water at a time.

      A. implausible   B. gaunt   C. blatant   D. nominal

_____ 8. Movie subtitles should be ___ with the spoken words they are translating.

      A. immaculate   B. hypothetical   C. incoherent   D. concurrent

_____ 9. Even the most ___ people have microscopic creatures clinging to their hair.

      A. sinister   B. immaculate   C. incoherent   D. intricate

_____ 10. A power failure ___ our viewing of the TV mystery, so we never found out who had committed the murder.

      A. deciphered   B. curtailed   C. retaliated   D. speculated

(Continues on next page)

PART B

On the answer line, write the letter of the choice that best completes each item.

_____ 11. Many men try to make themselves look more **virile** by
    A. eating more fruits and vegetables.   C. making quilts.
    B. learning to play a musical instrument.   D. lifting weights.

_____ 12. Which of the following **constitutes** a good breakfast?
    A. A neighborhood diner
    B. Orange juice and bran flakes with milk and bananas
    C. Spaghetti with anchovy sauce
    D. Customers at a pancake house

_____ 13. Since she wanted to **gloat** about her promotion at work, Kris
    A. didn't mention it to anyone.
    B. worked harder than ever to show that she deserved it.
    C. said to a coworker, "Sorry, loser. I got it."
    D. became very nervous about her new responsibilities.

_____ 14. In his lecture about television, the speaker **digressed** by
    A. mentioning a game-show series.
    B. saying, "Good morning. My topic today is television."
    C. discussing a soccer game he had seen the night before.
    D. examining television ads aimed at children.

_____ 15. Carmen's face showed **revulsion** as she listened to the speaker talk about
    A. exactly what happens to a person's body as he is electrocuted.
    B. the gourmet appetizers, meals, and desserts served on the cruise ship.
    C. advances in spinal-cord research that hold great promise for accident victims.
    D. financial-aid packages available to incoming college freshmen.

_____ 16. A usual **prerequisite** to getting a driver's license is
    A. purchasing a car.   C. passing a driving test.
    B. committing many traffic offenses.   D. refusing to have one's photograph taken.

_____ 17. When her brother and sister argue, Rachel often **intercedes** by
    A. leaving the house.   C. ignoring them both.
    B. covering her ears.   D. helping each see the other's point of view.

_____ 18. College students who don't eat properly and don't get much sleep are **vulnerable** to
    A. good health.   C. driving places.
    B. their doctors.   D. illness.

_____ 19. The parrot **garbled** its words,
    A. making us all laugh at its mixed-up speech.   C. embarrassing us with its dirty words.
    B. amazing us by speaking so clearly.   D. boring us by repeating the same few words.

_____ 20. The enormously successful movie _Titanic_ **incorporated**
    A. many millions of dollars.
    B. an ocean liner which struck an iceberg.
    C. elements of romance, adventure, and tragedy.
    D. Leonardo DiCaprio.

Score   (Number correct) _____ x 5 = _____ %

Enter your score above and in the **Vocabulary Performance Chart** on the inside back cover of the book.

PART A

Complete each item with a word from the box. Use each word once.

A. alleviate	B. benefactor	C. decipher	D. devastate	E. nominal
F. qualm	G. recession	H. retaliate	I. rigor	J. scrutiny
K. sinister	L. succumb	M. suffice		

_____ 1. Jesse had ___s about letting his cousin write his essay. "It's supposed to be my own work," he said.

_____ 2. Jill was ____(e)d when she lost her job and, with it, her hopes of affording a house.

_____ 3. The high school's chief ___ has offered to pay all college costs for any low-income student who graduates from the school.

_____ 4. Before the turn of the century, the ___s of prizefighting included boxing without gloves.

_____ 5. City Council ___(e)d to public pressure and passed a law that made smoking in restaurants illegal.

_____ 6. My brother hid hot peppers in my hamburgers, so I ___(e)d by putting salt in his coffee.

_____ 7. One of the oddest ___ plots of all time was thought up by a wealthy Frenchman. He fed his victims rich foods until they died of overeating.

_____ 8. The muscle ointment will ___ the pain of your sprained neck.

_____ 9. I don't know who sent me the birthday card because I couldn't ___ the signature.

_____ 10. A shortage of a single product, such as sugar, could cause a(n) ___ in several industries.

_____ 11. Don't buy a used car unless you examine it closely and also have a mechanic give it careful ___.

_____ 12. Although our library charges only a ___ fee to use its printers, I don't think it should charge students any fee at all.

_____ 13. "A hint to my daughter to take out the garbage won't ___," Alonso insisted. "She needs to be told to do it."

(Continues on next page)

PART B

Write **C** if the italicized word is used **correctly**. Write **I** if the word is used **incorrectly**.

_____ 14. The desire to aid others seems *intrinsic* to many animals. Baboons, for example, will try to free other baboons that are caged.

_____ 15. In a *blatant* case of injustice, a wealthy and influential North Carolina man received no punishment when he was caught selling drugs.

_____ 16. The Democratic and Republican parties are *predominant* in the United States, but other parties are also represented on the ballots.

_____ 17. A wonderfully *incoherent* speaker, Abraham Lincoln was widely admired for his powerful speeches.

_____ 18. Shortly before his birthday, Hollis *contrived* to get his parents to walk past the toy store so that he could point out the new XBox game system displayed in the window.

_____ 19. In ancient Rome, the huge stadium known as the Coliseum was a *sanctuary* where athletes fought each other to the death.

_____ 20. For two weeks, the newspapers reported on the crimes of the *infamous* serial killer.

_____ 21. Elise enjoys *intricate* jigsaw puzzles, such as those of detailed flower displays.

_____ 22. Fran often *squanders* her money by walking through rain or snow instead of paying for a cab.

_____ 23. A computer is *indispensable* for preparing a college term paper.

_____ 24. Felix's teacher suspected him of *plagiarism* because his last paper was so much better written than his others.

_____ 25. Each year, thousands of Americans who think themselves too *gaunt* have some fat surgically removed.

Score   (Number correct) _____ x 4 = _____%

PART A: Synonyms

In the space provided, write the letter of the choice that is most nearly the **same** in meaning as the **boldfaced** word.

_____ 1. **default**   A. upset greatly   B. plan   C. aid   D. fail to do something required

_____ 2. **revulsion**   A. charm   B. disgust   C. encouragement   D. something that weakens

_____ 3. **decipher**   A. interpret   B. think up   C. relieve   D. turn aside

_____ 4. **retaliate**   A. follow   B. cut short   C. pay back   D. disappoint greatly

_____ 5. **nominal**   A. necessary   B. obvious   C. evil   D. slight

_____ 6. **qualm**   A. doubt of conscience   B. inspection   C. requirement   D. demand

_____ 7. **concurrent**   A. most noticeable   B. complicated   C. weak   D. existing together

_____ 8. **intrinsic**   A. manly   B. wicked   C. natural   D. open to injury

_____ 9. **recession**   A. vacation   B. requirement   C. delay   D. business decline

_____ 10. **intercede**   A. disappoint   B. give in   C. come between   D. delay

_____ 11. **scrutiny**   A. inspection   B. moral strength   C. destruction   D. neglect

_____ 12. **contrive**   A. continue   B. think up   C. cut short   D. believe

_____ 13. **rigor**   A. energy   B. purpose   C. difficulty   D. harm

_____ 14. **sanctuary**   A. encouragement   B. shelter   C. requirement   D. decline

_____ 15. **covert**   A. necessary   B. slight   C. natural   D. secret

_____ 16. **benefactor**   A. villain   B. entertainer   C. helper   D. owner

_____ 17. **alleviate**   A. take   B. relieve   C. repay   D. build

_____ 18. **intermittent**   A. off-and-on   B. within   C. perfectly clean   D. complex

_____ 19. **digress**   A. be the parts of   B. turn aside   C. read   D. guess

_____ 20. **plagiarism**   A. correction   B. distaste   C. failure   D. stealing another's writings

_____ 21. **confiscate**   A. seize   B. interpret   C. make up   D. waste

_____ 22. **garble**   A. respond   B. pay back   C. relieve   D. scramble

_____ 23. **constitute**   A. seize   B. coexist   C. form   D. assume

_____ 24. **prerequisite**   A. cause   B. requirement   C. encouragement   D. difficulty

_____ 25. **speculate**   A. notice   B. theorize   C. give in to   D. combine

(Continues on next page)

PART B: Antonyms

In the space provided, write the letter of the choice that is most nearly the **opposite** in meaning to the **boldfaced** word.

_____ 26. **cynic**   A. enemy   B. optimist   C. patient person   D. expert

_____ 27. **demise**   A. failure   B. youth   C. conclusion   D. birth

_____ 28. **blight**   A. benefit   B. peace   C. increase   D. friendliness

_____ 29. **incentive**   A. improvement   B. mix-up   C. failure   D. discouragement

_____ 30. **gloat**   A. express regret   B. misinterpret   C. forget   D. resist

_____ 31. **degenerate**   A. command   B. give   C. try   D. improve

_____ 32. **indispensable**   A. perfectly clean   B. large   C. protected   D. unnecessary

_____ 33. **implausible**   A. common   B. believable   C. righteous   D. inspiring

_____ 34. **predominant**   A. uncommon   B. complicated   C. strong   D. early

_____ 35. **blatant**   A. serious   B. unnatural   C. unnoticeable   D. beneficial

_____ 36. **intricate**   A. encouraging   B. at fault   C. simple   D. unsteady

_____ 37. **devastate**   A. comfort   B. educate   C. admit   D. continue

_____ 38. **infamous**   A. believable   B. young   C. alive   D. honorably famous

_____ 39. **curtail**   A. improve   B. extend   C. admit   D. beautify

_____ 40. **incoherent**   A. quiet   B. well-known   C. logical   D. friendly

_____ 41. **virile**   A. homely   B. unnatural   C. graceful   D. feminine

_____ 42. **succumb**   A. resist   B. attract   C. learn   D. delay

_____ 43. **incorporate**   A. separate   B. do openly   C. add to   D. lose

_____ 44. **vulnerable**   A. clear   B. right   C. complete   D. protected

_____ 45. **sinister**   A. small   B. good   C. humorous   D. simple

_____ 46. **hypothetical**   A. real   B. constant   C. separate   D. unnatural

_____ 47. **gaunt**   A. optimistic   B. well   C. plump   D. short

_____ 48. **squander**   A. use wisely   B. ignore   C. become confused   D. continue

_____ 49. **immaculate**   A. confused   B. good   C. filthy   D. slight

_____ 50. **suffice**   A. plan   B. be not enough   C. be just right   D. give

Score   (Number correct) _____ x 2 = _____ %

Enter your score above and in the **Vocabulary Performance Chart** on the inside back cover of the book.

Each item below starts with a pair of words in CAPITAL LETTERS. For each item, figure out the relationship between these two words. Then decide which of the choices (A, B, C, or D. expresses a similar relationship. Write the letter of your choice on the answer line.

_____ 1. IMPLAUSIBLE : UNLIKELY ::
  A. straight : crooked
  B. unfortunate : unlucky
  C. furniture : house
  D. unfortunate : lucky

_____ 2. SANCTUARY : SAFETY ::
  A. hideout : secrecy
  B. enclosed : exposed
  C. wheel : steer
  D. dinner : breakfast

_____ 3. GAUNT : PLUMP ::
  A. tall : short
  B. thin : skinny
  C. precious : jewelry
  D. fruit : nutrition

_____ 4. BLIGHT : DESTROYS ::
  A. flood : dries
  B. medicine : heals
  C. pianist : piano
  D. agreement : disagree

_____ 5. DECIPHER : CODE ::
  A. surgeon : doctor
  B. untangle : knot
  C. puzzle : piece
  D. evident : clear

_____ 6. CONFISCATE : SEIZE ::
  A. confuse : clarify
  B. cry : funeral
  C. take : give
  D. contribute : give

_____ 7. HYPOTHETICAL : ACTUAL ::
  A. brave : cowardly
  B. scary : frightening
  C. old : ancient
  D. problem : solve

_____ 8. DEFAULT : LOAN ::
  A. pass : course
  B. pay : salary
  C. break : promise
  D. tax : income

_____ 9. INTRICATE : COMPLEX ::
  A. difficult : simple
  B. headlight : car
  C. circular : round
  D. scold : soothe

_____ 10. DEGENERATE : IMPROVE ::
  A. solve : equation
  B. generous : giving
  C. ride : train
  D. grow : shrink

(Continues on next page)

_____ 11. BENEFACTOR : SUPPORTS ::
      A. surgeon : operates   C. soldier : helmet
      B. leader : follows   D. waiter : waitress

_____ 12. CYNIC : OPTIMISTIC ::
      A. cucumber : vegetable   C. outcast : excluded
      B. criminal : law-abiding   D. ballerina : graceful

_____ 13. VIRILE : FEMININE ::
      A. manly : macho   C. popular : celebrity
      B. apartment : dwelling   D. fashionable : outmoded

_____ 14. INTERMITTENT : STEADY ::
      A. fortunate : unlucky   C. wise : advice
      B. treacherous : dishonest   D. instrument : violin

_____ 15. SPECULATE : THEORY ::
      A. speak : silent   C. draw : picture
      B. primary : secondary   D. manual : electronic

_____ 16. QUALM : CONSCIENCE ::
      A. love : hatred   C. cramp : muscle
      B. room : fireplace   D. pain : health

_____ 17. PLAGIARISM : IDEAS ::
      A. criminal : crime   C. writing : paper
      B. host : party   D. shoplifting : merchandise

_____ 18. CURTAIL : SHORTEN ::
      A. seek : find   C. silence : conversation
      B. depart : arrive   D. ask : inquire

_____ 19. DEVASTATE : DISASTER ::
      A. harm : nurse   C. bore : surprise
      B. amaze : miracle   D. cold : snow

_____ 20. INCENTIVE : MONEY ::
      A. youth : adulthood   C. vehicle : motorcycle
      B. cash : poverty   D. sanitation worker : garbage

Score   (Number correct) _____ x 5 = _____%

Unit Three

Chapter 11

abstain	deficit
affiliate	dissent
agnostic	diversion
aspire	lucrative
benevolent	mandatory

Chapter 12

charisma	poignant
contemporary	prevalent
contend	proponent
conversely	quest
extrovert	traumatic

Chapter 13

congenial	prone
flippant	rapport
impasse	rationale
perception	relentless
prompt	reprisal

Chapter 14

averse	endow
detract	expulsion
disdain	mortify
divulge	nullify
elation	ominous

Chapter 15

commemorate	empathy
complacent	menial
consensus	niche
deplete	transcend
diligent	waive

abstain	deficit
affiliate	dissent
agnostic	diversion
aspire	lucrative
benevolent	mandatory

Ten Words in Context

In the space provided, write the letter of the meaning closest to that of each **boldfaced** word. Use the context of the sentences to help you figure out each word's meaning.

1 abstain
(ăb-stān′)
-verb

● Although Luis has given up high-calorie desserts, he doesn't **abstain** completely from chocolate. He allows himself one small square of a Hershey bar a day.

● Many followers of Islam **abstain** from drinking alcohol or eating pork.

___ *Abstain from* means   A. to desire.   B. to believe in.   C. to deny oneself.

2 affiliate
(ə-fĭl′ē-āt′)
-verb

● Diane is neither a Democrat nor a Republican. She isn't **affiliated** with any political party.

● The young singer could have earned more if she had been **affiliated** with the musicians' union, but she couldn't afford the membership dues.

___ *Affiliate* means   A. to join.   B. to study.   C. to hold back.

3 agnostic
(ăg-nŏs′tĭk)
-noun

● Iris believes there is a God, and Marcia feels sure there isn't. Jean, an **agnostic**, feels that we can't be certain one way or the other.

● My uncle, who was an **agnostic**, used to say, "Humans cannot understand a flower, let alone whether or not there's a God."

___ *Agnostic* means   A. one who denies God's existence.   B. one who feels we can't know if God exists.   C. one who is sure there is a God.

4 aspire
(ə-spīr′)
-verb

● Twelve-year-old Derek, who loves drawing buildings, **aspires** to be an architect.

● Millions of young people **aspire** to be professional athletes, but only a few will succeed.

___ *Aspire* means   A. to fear.   B. to wish.   C. to volunteer.

5 benevolent
(bə-nĕv′ə-lənt)
-adjective

● People are more **benevolent** at Christmas, the "season for giving."

● In 1878, William Booth founded a **benevolent** association to help the poor of London. He called it the Salvation Army.

___ *Benevolent* means   A. recreational.   B. profitable.   C. charitable.

6 deficit
(dĕf′ə-sĭt)
-noun

● Our club has spent much more money than it has taken in, so it now has a huge budget **deficit**.

● Residents are asked not to water their lawns because a **deficit** of rain has dangerously lowered the water supply.

___ *Deficit* means   A. a lack.   B. an overflow.   C. a collection.

7 dissent
(dĭ-sĕnt′)
-noun

● The committee was so torn by **dissent** that its members could not even agree on whether or not to schedule another meeting.

● The dictator permitted people to agree with his policies or keep silent about them, but not to express **dissent**.

___ *Dissent* means   A. plans.   B. opposition.   C. relief.

8 diversion
(də-vûr′zhən)
-noun

● My history teacher says that one of her favorite **diversions** during summer vacation is reading mystery novels.

● Skip likes his job, but he also enjoys such **diversions** as playing video games, watching baseball, and reading humorous stories.

___ *Diversion* means   A. a way to relax.   B. something easy.   C. an assignment.

9 lucrative
(loo′krə-tĭv)
-adjective

● The Girl Scout cookie stand was more **lucrative** than anyone expected. It raised almost $500 in one afternoon!

● "Working in an animal shelter isn't the most **lucrative** job," Ms. Baum admitted, "but I've never felt the need to make lots of money."

___ *Lucrative* means   A. required.   B. financially rewarding.   C. risky.

10 mandatory
(măn′də-tôr′ē)
-adjective

● Members of the basketball team have to follow strict rules. For example, it's **mandatory** that each player attend at least 80 percent of the practices.

● "A research paper isn't **mandatory**," the instructor said, "but if you write one, you'll get extra credit."

___ *Mandatory* means   A. unimportant.   B. helpful.   C. essential.

Matching Words with Definitions

Following are definitions of the ten words. Clearly write or print each word next to its definition. The sentences above and on the previous page will help you decide on the meaning of each word.

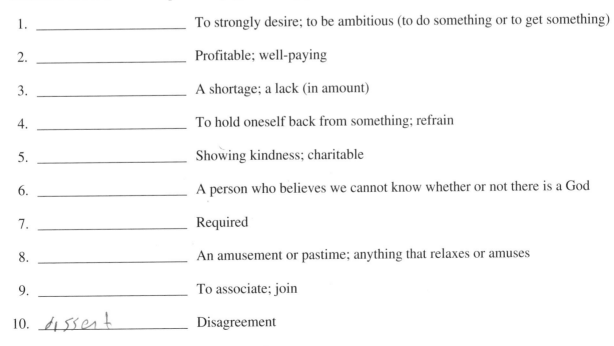

1. _____ To strongly desire; to be ambitious (to do something or to get something)

2. _____ Profitable; well-paying

3. _____ A shortage; a lack (in amount)

4. _____ To hold oneself back from something; refrain

5. _____ Showing kindness; charitable

6. _____ A person who believes we cannot know whether or not there is a God

7. _____ Required

8. _____ An amusement or pastime; anything that relaxes or amuses

9. _____ To associate; join

10. ___dissent___ Disagreement

CAUTION: Do not go any further until you are sure the above answers are correct. Then you can use the definitions to help you in the following practices. Your goal is eventually to know the words well enough so that you don't need to check the definitions at all.

Sentence Check 1

Using the answer line provided, complete each item below with the correct word from the box. Use each word once.

| A. **abstain** | B. **affiliate** | C. **agnostic** | D. **aspire** | E. **benevolent** |
| F. **deficit** | G. **dissent** | H. **diversion** | I. **lucrative** | J. **mandatory** |

_____ 1. Because Hank needs to lose weight, his doctor recommended that he ___ from all sweets and fatty foods.

_____ 2. An entrance fee wasn't ___, but a sign at the museum entrance suggested that visitors make a donation.

_____ 3. My sister enjoys taking walks and going shopping, but I prefer such ___s as listening to music or curling up with a good book.

_____ 4. The ___ fund at my church collects money to help needy families in our parish.

_____ 5. My kid brother ___s to become the video-game champion of the world.

_____ 6. Acting is ___ for only a small percentage of performers. The rest need additional sources of income, such as waiting on tables or parking cars.

_____ 7. "When someone who believes in God marries someone who does not," the comic asked, "do they give birth to a(n) ___?"

_____ 8. Yong could have joined the all-male club, but he prefers to ___ with organizations that welcome both men and women.

_____ 9. There was no ___ in the family on whether or not to start a vegetable garden this year. We all agreed it was a great idea.

_____ 10. We could overcome a(n) ___ of organs for transplants if more people would agree to have their organs donated after they die.

NOTE: Now check your answers to these items by turning to page 130. Going over the answers carefully will help you prepare for the next two practices, for which answers are not given.

Sentence Check 2

Using the answer lines provided, complete each item below with **two** words from the box. Use each word once.

agnostic
benevolent   1–2. Some people think that since Stan is a(n) ___, he must be amoral°. It's true he's not sure if God exists, but that doesn't mean he lacks a moral sense. In fact, he recently founded a ___ society at work to raise money for disabled children in the area.

abstain
mandatory   3–4. Gail didn't ___ from smoking cigarettes until her employer made not smoking ___. Keeping her job was a very good incentive° to get her to quit.

affiliate
diversion   5–6. My uncle decided to splurge and ___ with a country club because golf is his favorite ___.

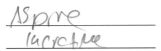

Aspire
lucrative

7–8. Because my father ___s to make enough money to send his children to college, he's working hard to make his auto repair business as ___ as possible.

dissent
deficit

9–10. The ___ in the township treasury is causing a lot of ___ over whether or not taxes should be raised.

Final Check: *Conflict Over Holidays*

Here is a final opportunity for you to strengthen your knowledge of the ten words. First read the following selection carefully. Then fill in each blank with a word from the box at the top of the previous page. (Context clues will help you figure out which word goes in which blank.) Use each word once.

While Jeanne and Paul are generally a happily married couple, they do struggle over one point of (1) *dissen* . They disagree as to how their family should observe religious holidays.

"The emphasis on presents," says Jeanne, "has made the season (2) *lucrative* for all those mercenary° retailers who overcharge at holiday time. Also, people who should be watching their expenses create unnecessary (3) *deficit* s in their budgets by squandering° money on unimportant gifts." She complains that exchanging presents at Christmas is practically (4) *mandatory* , whether or not one believes in the holiday's religious significance. Jeanne (5)_____s to keep her home free of all such nonreligious customs and thus wants her children to (6)_____ from traditions such as gift-giving and dyeing Easter eggs. She feels the family's money would be better spent if it were donated to a (7)_____ organization for helping the poor. Some of Jeanne's neighbors assume that she is a(n) (8)_____ because of her lack of holiday spirit. They are wrong, however. Jeanne believes deeply in God and is (9)_____(e)d with a church.

© vnlit/shutterstock.com

While Paul understands Jeanne's concerns, he prefers the conventional° way of celebrating holidays. "Children enjoy the customary (10)_____s that are connected with the holidays," he says. "What would Christmas be without a visit to Santa and gifts under the tree? What would Easter be without colorful eggs and an Easter egg hunt? These are pleasant practices that enhance° the joy of the season."

Scores   Sentence Check 2 _____%   Final Check _____%

charisma	poignant
contemporary	prevalent
contend	proponent
conversely	quest
extrovert	traumatic

Ten Words in Context

In the space provided, write the letter of the meaning closest to that of each **boldfaced** word. Use the context of the sentences to help you figure out each word's meaning.

1 charisma
(kə-rĭz′mə)
-noun

- Kamal has such **charisma** that when he ran for class president, almost every person in the tenth grade voted for him. His classmates couldn't resist Kamal's magnetic personality.
- Great Britain's Princess Diana obviously had great **charisma**. She continues to have numerous loyal fans—long after her death.

___ *Charisma* means   A. feelings.   B. personal appeal.   C. luck.

2 contemporary
(kən-tĕm′pə-rĕr′ē)
-adjective

- Beth likes **contemporary** furniture, but her husband prefers antiques.
- My grandfather says that compared to kids in his day, **contemporary** youngsters are soft and lazy.

___ *Contemporary* means   A. common.   B. old-fashioned.   C. today's.

3 contend
(kən-tĕnd′)
-verb

- The defense attorney **contended** that his client was insane and therefore could not be held responsible for the crime.
- Scientists **contend** that no two snowflakes are identical, but how could they possibly prove it?

___ *Contend* means   A. to wish.   B. to deny.   C. to declare.

4 conversely
(kən-vûrs′lē)
-adverb

- Ron, who is basically bored by food, eats in order to live. **Conversely**, Nate loves food so much that he seems to live in order to eat.
- Mary drives her children to school whenever it rains. **Conversely**, Thea makes her kids walk because she thinks a little rain never hurt anyone.

___ *Conversely* means   A. in contrast.   B. in a modern way.   C. similarly.

5 extrovert
(ĕk′strə-vûrt′)
-noun

- Surprisingly, not all performers are **extroverts**. Offstage, many are quiet and shy.
- Most politicians are **extroverts**; they enjoy being around people and talking with them constantly.

___ *Extrovert* means   A. a supporter of causes.   B. a timid person.   C. a sociable person.

6 poignant
(poin′yənt)
-adjective

- The service honoring American soldiers missing in action was touching. A speech by a friend of one of the soldiers was particularly **poignant**.
- I cried when I read a **poignant** story about a dying girl who gave away all of her dolls to "less fortunate children."

___ *Poignant* means   A. affecting the emotions.   B. correct.   C. lively.

7 prevalent
(prĕv′ə-lənt)
-adjective

- Unemployment was **prevalent** during America's Great Depression. By 1932, more than twelve million people were out of work.
- Televisions are more **prevalent** in the United States than bathtubs. Over half of American homes have three or more TVs. Far fewer homes have more than one bathtub.

___ *Prevalent* means   A. favorable.   B. found frequently.   C. unlikely.

8 proponent
(prō-pō′nənt)
-noun

- I voted for Senator Williams, a **proponent** of improved services for the elderly, because I feel that many older people need greater assistance.
- Although Elaine quit work to take care of her children, she is a **proponent** of employer-supported day care.

___ *Proponent* means   A. a recipient.   B. an opponent.   C. a supporter.

9 quest
(kwĕst)
-noun

- During Carlo's **quest** for the perfect pizza, he sampled the cheese pizza at twenty-seven different restaurants.
- Ponce de Leon's **quest** was for the Fountain of Youth; what he found instead was Florida.

___ *Quest* means   A. a hunt.   B. a question.   C. a design.

10 traumatic
(trô-măt′ĭk)
-adjective

- Divorce can be less **traumatic** for children if their fears and feelings are taken into account as the divorce takes place.
- My cousin has had nightmares ever since his **traumatic** experience of being trapped in a coal mine.

___ *Traumatic* means   A. familiar.   B. reasonable.   C. extremely upsetting.

Matching Words with Definitions

Following are definitions of the ten words. Clearly write or print each word next to its definition. The sentences above and on the previous page will help you decide on the meaning of each word.

1. _____ In an opposite manner; in an altogether different way

2. _____ The quality of a leader which captures great popular devotion; personal magnetism; charm

3. _____ A search; pursuit

4. _____ Widespread; common

5. _____ To state to be so; claim; affirm

6. _____ Modern; up-to-date

7. _____ Someone who supports a cause

8. _____ Emotionally moving; touching

9. _____ Causing painful emotions, with possible long-lasting psychological effects

10. _____ An outgoing, sociable person

CAUTION: Do not go any further until you are sure the above answers are correct. Then you can use the definitions to help you in the following practices. Your goal is eventually to know the words well enough so that you don't need to check the definitions at all.

Sentence Check 1

Using the answer line provided, complete each item below with the correct word from the box. Use each word once.

A. **charisma**	B. **contemporary**	C. **contend**	D. **conversely**	E. **extrovert**
F. **poignant**	G. **prevalent**	H. **proponent**	I. **quest**	J. **traumatic**

_____ 1. "This woman ___s that she was here before you," said the supermarket checkout clerk. "Is it her turn now?"

_____ 2. Underage drinking was so ___ in the fraternity house that college officials ordered the house closed for a year.

_____ 3. At the airport, I was very moved by the ___ reunion of family members who had been separated for years.

_____ 4. Nancy is a(n) ___ by nature, but since she's become depressed, she has avoided other people.

_____ 5. I study best in the morning. ___, my sister concentrates better at night.

_____ 6. During the past three hundred years, several people have gone on a(n) ___ for Noah's ark. Some have looked for it in northeastern Turkey, on Mount Ararat, sixteen thousand feet above sea level.

_____ 7. Repeating third grade was ___ for my brother. It still pains him to think about it, even though he's a successful businessman now.

_____ 8. Abby didn't like the apartment with the old-fashioned bathtub and radiators. She preferred a more ___ place.

_____ 9. Certain movie stars may not be great actors, but they have a(n) ___ that makes people want to see their films.

_____ 10. Felipe is a(n) ___ of exercising for good health. He even encourages his young children to swim or cycle every day.

NOTE: Now check your answers to these items by turning to page 130. Going over the answers carefully will help you prepare for the next two practices, for which answers are not given.

Sentence Check 2

Using the answer lines provided, complete each item below with **two** words from the box. Use each word once.

extrovert
conversely

1–2. Judy and Martin Reed exemplify° the old saying "Opposites attract." A(n) ___, Judy chooses work that brings her into constant contact with others. ___, Martin prefers jobs in which he mainly works alone.

prevalent
contemporary

3–4. Many people are surprised to learn how ___ poverty is in ___ America. Today, millions live below the poverty line, and the number seems to escalate° daily.

charisma

propret

5–6. Mahatma Gandhi's ___ and vision inspired millions of fellow Indians to join him enthusiastically in the ___ for peaceful solutions to national problems. Gandhi incorporated° nonviolence and political activism into a highly effective method for social change: passive resistance.

contod

poignant

7–8. My mother ___s that *Romeo and Juliet* is the most ___ story ever written, but my sister claims Erich Segal's *Love Story* is more moving.

poiand

propret

9–10. Ever since the ___ experience of finding her son dead from a drug overdose, Sophie has been a strong ___ of mandatory° drug education in the public schools. If drug education isn't required, she says, schools may cut corners and omit it.

Final Check: *Dr. Martin Luther King, Jr.*

Here is a final opportunity for you to strengthen your knowledge of the ten words. First read the following selection carefully. Then fill in each blank with a word from the box at the top of the previous page. (Context clues will help you figure out which word goes in which blank.) Use each word once.

(1)_____Contrary_____ young people may be able to list the many accomplishments of the Reverend Dr. Martin Luther King, Jr. They may know that he was a civil rights leader who aspired° to achieve racial harmony and was a(n) (2)_____ of peaceful but direct action. They may know that he fought the discrimination against blacks that was so (3)_____ in our country in the 1950s and 1960s. They may also know that

© public domain image per wunc.org

he received a great deal of acclaim° for his work. For example, in 1964 he won the Nobel Peace Prize. They may even (4)_____ that he is the most important social reformer in the history of our nation.

But can the young really know the (5)_____, the powerful personal magnetism of this man? He was a perfect blend of quiet, considerate thinker and bold, outspoken (6)_____. When Dr. King spoke, people listened. He had such a forceful yet (7)_____ way of speaking that those who heard him felt his message deep within. For most, this meant a stronger belief in and respect for the man and his ideals. (8)_____, for bigots, it meant hatred and fear of what he stood for.

Dr. King's (9)_____ for equal rights for all was clear when he said, "I have a dream that this nation will rise up and live out the true meaning of its creed: 'We hold these truths to be self-evident; that all men are created equal.'" He gave his time, his leadership, and, in the end, his life. His murder was a (10)_____ event in the lives of many Americans, who never fully recovered from that awful day. But because of Martin Luther King, Americans live with greater dignity. And many have taken up his fight against the injustice of racism.

Scores	Sentence Check 2 _____ %	Final Check _____ %

congenial	prone
flippant	rapport
impasse	rationale
perception	relentless
prompt	reprisal

Ten Words in Context

In the space provided, write the letter of the meaning closest to that of each **boldfaced** word. Use the context of the sentences to help you figure out each word's meaning.

1 congenial
(kən-jēn′yəl)
-*adjective*

● I was nervous being at a party where I didn't know anyone, but the other guests were so **congenial** that I soon felt at ease.

● Most people don't realize pigs can be great pets. Like dogs, they are generally warm, gentle, and **congenial** animals.

___ *Congenial* means   A. persistent.   B. intelligent.   C. friendly.

2 flippant
(flĭp′ənt)
-*adjective*

● "Don't give me a **flippant** answer," George's father told him. "Your financial situation is a serious matter."

● When a teenage boy is asked to clean his room, he's likely to give a **flippant** response such as "Why should I? I just cleaned it last month."

___ *Flippant* means   A. rude.   B. serious.   C. incorrect.

3 impasse
(ĭm′pǎs)
-*noun*

● The jurors had reached an **impasse**. They couldn't agree on a verdict—some thought the defendant was the murderer, but others were sure he was innocent.

● If you think you've reached an **impasse** when trying to solve a problem, take a break. The solution may occur to you while you're doing something else.

___ *Impasse* means   A. a deadlock.   B. a relationship.   C. an opportunity.

4 perception
(pər-sĕp′shən)
-*noun*

● Brenda's **perceptions** of others are usually accurate. She is a good judge of character.

● "Our **perceptions** of our problem differ," Tonya explained. "Sam thinks money is the main issue, but I believe it's a question of who controls the purse strings."

___ *Perception* means   A. a memory.   B. a view.   C. a desire.

5 prompt
(prŏmpt)
-*verb*

● To **prompt** her son to go back to school, Mrs. Davis left a stack of college brochures on his pillow.

● Fast-food clerks **prompt** customers to spend more money by asking such questions as "Would you like cookies or apple pie with that?"

___ *Prompt* means   A. to allow.   B. to agree with.   C. to encourage.

6 prone
(prōn)
-*adjective*

● Mr. Walker is **prone** to sleep problems, so he limits his intake of caffeine.

● **Prone** to fits of laughter during class, Chris controls himself by chewing on his pen.

___ *Prone* means   A. tending.   B. immune.   C. attracted.

76

7 rapport
(ră-pŏr′)
-noun

- In high school, I had such good **rapport** with my gym teacher that our close relationship continues to this day.
- If no **rapport** develops between you and your therapist after a month or two, start looking for a counselor who makes you feel comfortable.

___ *Rapport* means   A. a report.   (B.) a personal connection.   C. a financial situation.

8 rationale
(răsh′ə-năl′)
-noun

- Danielle's **rationale** for majoring in business was simple. She said, "I want to make a lot of money."
- The **rationale** for not lowering the drinking age to 18 is that self-control and good judgment are still being developed at that age.

___ *Rationale* means   A. a situation.   (B.) an explanation.   C. a question.

impressont

9 relentless
(rĭ-lĕnt′lĭs)
-adjective

- The dog's **relentless** barking got on my nerves. He barked the entire two hours his owners were out.
- In a large city, the noise of crowds and heavy traffic is so **relentless** that it can be difficult to find peace and quiet.

___ *Relentless* means   A. occasional.   B. exciting.   (C.) nonstop.

10 reprisal
(rĭ-prī′zəl)
-noun

- In **reprisal** for being fired, the troubled man filled his Facebook page with lies about his former boss.
- Fear of **reprisal** may keep children from telling parents or teachers about a bully who has threatened them.

___ *Reprisal* means   A. disrespect.   (B.) revenge.   C. delay.

Matching Words with Definitions

Following are definitions of the ten words. Clearly write or print each word next to its definition. The sentences above and on the previous page will help you decide on the meaning of each word.

1. _____ Insight or understanding gained through observation; impression

2. _____ Having a tendency; inclined (to do something)

3. _____ Persistent; continuous

4. _____ The underlying reasons for something; logical basis

5. _____ Disrespectful and not serious enough

6. _____ Agreeable or pleasant in character; friendly; sociable

7. _____ To urge into action; motivate

8. _____ The paying back of one injury or bad deed with another

9. _____ A situation with no way out; dead end

10. _____ Relationship, especially one that is close, trusting, or sympathetic

CAUTION: Do not go any further until you are sure the above answers are correct. Then you can use the definitions to help you in the following practices. Your goal is eventually to know the words well enough so that you don't need to check the definitions at all.

Sentence Check 1

Using the answer line provided, complete each item below with the correct word from the box. Use each word once.

A. congenial	B. flippant	C. impasse	D. perception	E. prompt
F. prone	G. rapport	H. rationale	I. relentless	J. reprisal

_____ 1. There was instant ___ between Duke and Otis. They talked as if they'd known each other for years.

_____ 2. It took his best friend's heart attack to ___ my dad to start exercising and eating right.

_____ 3. My brother hides his lack of confidence by being ___. He rarely treats anything seriously.

_____ 4. You will get along better in life if you are ___ to other people, rather than unpleasant.

_____ 5. Raquel is ___ to accidents, so her car insurance rates are quite high.

_____ 6. The ___ behind encouraging pregnant women to gain about twenty-five pounds is that low weight gain can lead to dangerously low birth weights.

_____ 7. When Lacey and John divorced, she tried to get more than half his income. In ___, he tried not to give her any of his income at all.

_____ 8. Floyd's ___ of human nature is strongly colored by some bad experiences. He thinks everyone is basically selfish.

_____ 9. During April and May, the rain was so ___ that we thought we might have to trade in our car for a boat.

_____ 10. At the movie's turning point, the bad guys reached a(n) ___. On one side of them was the police; on the other was a steep cliff.

NOTE: Now check your answers to these items by turning to page 130. Going over the answers carefully will help you prepare for the next two practices, for which answers are not given.

Sentence Check 2

Using the answer lines provided, complete each item below with **two** words from the box. Use each word once.

rationale
prompt

1–2. Although the company president explained the ___ behind the pay cuts, his announcement ___(e)d an employee protest. However, once it was learned that the president was also taking a big pay cut, the employees' dissent° died down.

congenial
rapport

3–4. Because Wade is so ___ and easy to talk to, we established a warm ___ the first day we met.

relentless
reprisal

5–6. Alma could put up with occasional kidding, but her brother's teasing was often ___, going on for weeks at a time. Sick of it all, she finally planned a(n) ___ that would embarrass him in front of his friends.

perception
impasse

7–8. My ___ of the situation is that talks between the factory management and union officials reached a(n) ___ because neither side would compromise on salary increases and health benefits. In such situations, flexibility is a prerequisite° to progress.

prompt
flippant

9–10. The waitresses in our local diner are ___ to be funny and not always polite. If a customer says, "I'm ready to order now," he may get a ___ response such as, "And I'm ready to retire, but you don't hear me making a big deal about it."

Final Check: _Relating to Parents_

Here is a final opportunity for you to strengthen your knowledge of the ten words. First read the following selection carefully. Then fill in each blank with a word from the box at the top of the previous page. (Context clues will help you figure out which word goes in which blank.) Use each word once.

© CREATISTA/shutterstock.com

How do you respond when your parents deny you permission to do something? For example, if you want to travel and work around the country for the summer, but your parents say you're too young, do you become furious and angrily demand that they stop curtailing° your rights? Do you plan a(n) (1)_____, vowing to ruin their summer plans because they've ruined yours? Or do you explain the (2)_____ behind your request, so that your parents will understand your reasoning?

The way you behave when you and your parents reach a(n) (3)_____ on an issue can have a big effect on how they view you. Sure, you could reply, "Fine. I'll go buy a leash so you can really run my life." But if you are consistently (4)_____ like that, you'll just strengthen their (5)_____ of you as being too immature to be on your own. Also, if you are (6)_____ in your begging, asking them three hundred times a day, "But _why_ won't you let me travel alone?" you might elicit° this response: "You may do some traveling alone right now—go directly to your room."

Instead, approach your parents in a (7)_____ way and try to develop a strong, friendly (8)_____ with them. An amiable°, respectful relationship will make them more (9)_____ to see things your way. Even if you can't (10)_____ them to change their minds about this summer's plans, your chances of getting their support will be better the next time you want to try something new.

Scores   Sentence Check 2 _____%   Final Check _____%

CHAPTER

14

averse	endow
detract	expulsion
disdain	mortify
divulge	nullify
elation	ominous

Ten Words in Context

In the space provided, write the letter of the meaning closest to that of each **boldfaced** word. Use the context of the sentences to help you figure out each word's meaning.

1 averse
(ə-vûrs′)
-*adjective*

decrecer

● That little boy was once so **averse** to tomatoes that the very sight of them made him gag.

● Being **averse** to screaming crowds, I'd rather just listen to music at home than go to a live concert.

___ *Averse* means   A. opposed.   B. accustomed.   C. open.

2 detract
(dĭ-trăkt′)
-*verb*

● Julius thinks the scar on his cheek **detracts** from his good looks, but it's barely noticeable.

● All of the litter in the park certainly **detracts** from the beauty of the trees and flowers.

___ *Detract* means   A. to result.   B. to benefit.   C. to take away.

despreo

3 disdain
(dĭs-dān′)
-*noun*

● The snobby server in the French restaurant viewed Tanya with **disdain** because she couldn't pronounce anything on the menu.

● I was afraid my request to see the state senator would be treated with **disdain**. Instead, the senator's secretary politely made an appointment for me.

___ *Disdain* means   A. pride.   B. disrespect.   C. sorrow.

4 divulge
(dĭ-vŭlj′)
-*verb*

● My father wouldn't **divulge** the type of car he had bought, saying only, "It's a surprise."

● It's against the law to ask people to **divulge** their age at a job interview.

___ *Divulge* means   A. to hide.   B. to recall.   C. to tell.

5 elation
(ĭ-lā′shən)
-*noun*

● The principal shouted with **elation** when the football team scored the winning touchdown.

● Roy had expected to feel **elation** at his graduation. Instead, he felt sadness at the thought of not seeing his high-school friends every day.

___ *Elation* means   A. anger.   B. confusion.   C. happiness.

dotado

6 endow
(ĕn-dou′)
-*verb*

● Nature has **endowed** hummingbirds with the ability to fly backward.

● The author Oscar Wilde was **endowed** with the ability to find humor in any situation. While dying, he said of the ugly wallpaper in his room, "One of us had to go."

___ *Endow* means   A. to equip.   B. to curse.   C. to threaten.

7 expulsion
(ĕks-pŭl′shən)
-noun

● The manager told us we risked **expulsion** from the theater if we continued to talk on our cell phones during the movie.

● **Expulsion** from school is supposed to be a punishment, but some students may consider not being allowed to attend classes a reward.

___ *Expulsion* means   A. being canceled.   B. being forced out.   C. being embarrassed.

guarantase

8 mortify
(môr′tə-fī′)
-verb

● It would **mortify** me if my voice cracked during my choir solo.

● I doubt anything will ever **mortify** me more than the streamer of toilet paper that clung to my shoe as I returned from the ladies' room to rejoin my date in a fancy restaurant.

___ *Mortify* means   A. to shame.   B. to insult.   C. to delay.

9 nullify
(nŭl′ə-fī′)
-verb

● The college will **nullify** my student ID at the end of the term unless I update it with a new sticker.

● A soft-drink company decided to **nullify** its contract with a well-known athlete because he was convicted of drunken driving.

___ *Nullify* means   A. to renew.   B. to reveal.   C. to cancel.

Amenazates.

10 ominous
(ŏm′ə-nəs)
-adjective

● To many, cemeteries have an **ominous** quality, particularly at night or on Halloween, when the threat of ghosts can seem very real.

● The sore's failure to heal was **ominous**, a possible sign of infection.

___ *Ominous* means   A. embarrassing.   B. threatening.   C. unworthy.

Matching Words with Definitions

Following are definitions of the ten words. Clearly write or print each word next to its definition. The sentences above and on the previous page will help you decide on the meaning of each word.

1. _____ To provide with a talent or quality

2. _____ An attitude or feeling of contempt; scorn

3. _____ The act or condition of being forced to leave

4. _____ Threatening harm or evil; menacing

5. _____ To reveal; make known

6. _____ Having a feeling of dislike or distaste for something

7. _____ To humiliate or embarrass

8. _____ To lessen what is admirable or worthwhile about something

9. _____ A feeling of great joy or pride

10. _____ To make legally ineffective; cancel

CAUTION: Do not go any further until you are sure the above answers are correct. Then you can use the definitions to help you in the following practices. Your goal is eventually to know the words well enough so that you don't need to check the definitions at all.

Sentence Check 1

Using the answer line provided, complete each item below with the correct word from the box. Use each word once.

A. averse	B. detract	C. disdain	D. divulge	E. elation
F. endow	G. expulsion	H. mortified	I. nullified	J. ominous

_____ 1. The results of the mayoral election were ___ after the townspeople found evidence of voting fraud.

_____ 2. When he received the college scholarship, my brother felt such ___ that he wept with joy.

_____ 3. I'm ___ to speaking in public because I don't enjoy making a fool of myself.

_____ 4. Because of the dark, ___ storm clouds, we canceled the softball game.

_____ 5. People talking in a movie theater greatly ___ from the enjoyment of watching a film.

_____ 6. The reporter was ___ when he learned that he had delivered much of his news story facing away from the TV camera.

_____ 7. Never trust Esta with a secret. She'll ___ it the minute you turn your back.

_____ 8. Vinnie's repeated boasts about his muscle-building backfired. They caused his date to look at him with ___, not admiration.

_____ 9. Russian athletes faced ___ from the Olympics when it was revealed that many were taking illegal drugs to improve their performance.

_____ 10. The American water shrew is ___(e)d with feet that have air pockets, enabling the small animal to walk on water.

NOTE: Now check your answers to these items by turning to page 130. Going over the answers carefully will help you prepare for the next two practices, for which answers are not given.

Sentence Check 2

Using the answer lines provided, complete each item below with **two** words from the box. Use each word once.

_____divulge_____
_____expulsion_____   1–2. When someone ___(e)d to a counselor that a certain student was selling drugs, an investigation began that led to that student's ___ from school.

_____endow_____
_____   3–4. Shannon is ___(e)d with beautiful curly red hair, but her self-image is so low that she feels her hair ___s from her looks. However, others find her hair to be one of her many attractive physical attributes°.

_____averse_____
_____   5–6. Some people are so ___ to living near a nuclear plant that they want the plant's license to be ___. They say the plant violates every homeowner's right to safety.

_____

_____   7–8. Marty had believed his headaches and blurred vision were ___ signs of some terrible syndrome°, so he felt ___ when he learned that he simply needed glasses.

_____

_____   9–10. Amy was ___ by the low grade she received for her speech, a grade she considered a sign of the teacher's ___ for her. However, the teacher's rationale° for the grade was that the speech was incoherent°.

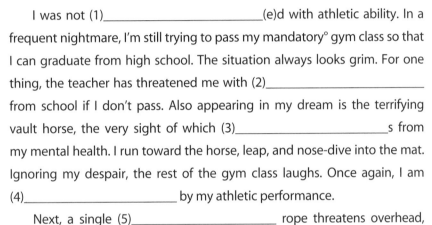

Final Check: *The Nightmare of Gym*

Here is a final opportunity for you to strengthen your knowledge of the ten words. First read the following selection carefully. Then fill in each blank with a word from the box at the top of the previous page. (Context clues will help you figure out which word goes in which blank.) Use each word once.

I was not (1)_____(e)d with athletic ability. In a frequent nightmare, I'm still trying to pass my mandatory° gym class so that I can graduate from high school. The situation always looks grim. For one thing, the teacher has threatened me with (2)_____ from school if I don't pass. Also appearing in my dream is the terrifying vault horse, the very sight of which (3)_____s from my mental health. I run toward the horse, leap, and nose-dive into the mat. Ignoring my despair, the rest of the gym class laughs. Once again, I am (4)_____ by my athletic performance.

© Polhansen/shutterstock.com

Next, a single (5)_____ rope threatens overhead, where it hangs from the ceiling. I try to contrive° some excuse to get out of climbing it. However, my excuses are so incoherent° that my teacher says, "I don't understand anything you're saying. Get started." Wondering if anyone has ever died from rope burn, I struggle to climb it. Barely halfway up, I sweat so much that I slide back to the floor, landing at the gym teacher's feet. "What a loser," the teacher mutters with an expression of total (6)_____.

Because I've always been (7)_____ to square-dancing, that too appears in the nightmare. Having forgotten my sneakers, I'm forced to dance in my socks. I slip, rather than dance, around the polished floor. During one high-speed turn, I go sliding—right into the men's locker room, where the smell causes me to pass out.

The only pleasant part of the dream comes near the end. With amazement and (8)_____, I learn that I will graduate after all. I smile, thinking I'll never have to face the rigors° of gym class again.

But then, the principal (9)_____s the terrible truth. I haven't managed to pass gym. My graduation depends on my agreeing to take four more years of gym when I get to college. If I don't, my high school diploma will be (10)_____.

Scores   Sentence Check 2 _____%   Final Check _____%

Enter your scores above and in the **Vocabulary Performance Chart** on the inside back cover of the book.

commemorate	empathy
complacent	menial
consensus	niche
deplete	transcend
diligent	waive

Ten Words in Context

In the space provided, write the letter of the meaning closest to that of each **boldfaced** word. Use the context of the sentences to help you figure out each word's meaning.

1 commemorate
(kə-měm′ə-rāt′)
-verb

● Thomas devoted himself to feeding the hungry. So on the anniversary of his death, it seems wrong to **commemorate** his life with a fancy dinner party that only the rich can attend.

● Each year, my parents **commemorate** their first date by having dinner at McDonalds, the place where they first met.

___ *Commemorate* means   A. to share.   B. to celebrate.   C. to believe.

2 complacent
(kəm-plā′sənt)
-adjective

● Elected officials cannot afford to be **complacent** about winning an election. Before long, they'll have to campaign again for the voters' support.

● Getting all A's hasn't made Ivy **complacent**. She continues to work hard at school.

___ *Complacent* means   A. very eager.   B. reasonable.   C. too much at ease.

consenso

3 consensus
(kən-sěn′səs)
-noun

● A vote revealed strong agreement among the teachers. The **consensus** was that they would strike if the school board did not act quickly to raise their pay.

● The family **consensus** was that we should go camping again this summer. Ray was the only one who wanted to do something different.

___ *Consensus* means   A. a majority view.   B. an unusual idea.   C. a question.

reducir

4 deplete
(dĭ-plēt′)
-verb

● I'd like to help you out with a loan, but unexpected car repairs have managed to **deplete** my bank account.

● In order not to **deplete** their small supply of canned food, the shipwreck survivors searched the island for plants they could eat.

___ *Deplete* means   A. to use up.   B. to forget.   C. to find.

5 diligent
(dĭl′ə-jənt)
-adjective

● I wish I had been more **diligent** about practicing piano when I was younger. It would be nice to be able to play well now.

● George is a **diligent** chef. He is constantly working to improve his skills and make each meal he creates better than the one before.

___ *Diligent* means   A. self-satisfied.   B. lucky.   C. hard-working.

6 empathy
(ěm′pə-thē)
-noun

● Families who lost loved ones in the attacks on the World Trade Center and the Pentagon have **empathy** for one another because of their shared grief.

● Ms. Allan is an excellent career counselor partly because of her great **empathy**. She understands each student's feelings and point of view.

___ *Empathy* means   A. a common opinion.   B. a sympathetic understanding.   C. an efficiency.

Empatía
en conciencia

7 menial
(mē′nē-əl)
-adjective

- Julio seems to think my summer job delivering pizza is **menial** work, but I've found that it requires some skills.
- Every job can be done with pride. Even **menial** jobs such as washing windows or scrubbing floors can be performed with care.

___ *Menial* means   A. unskilled.   B. steady.   C. satisfying.

que no necesita una preparación

8 niche
(nĭch)
-noun

- Although her degree was in accounting, Kendra decided her **niche** was really in business management, so she went back to school for more training.
- Dom spent the years after college moving restlessly from job to job, never finding a comfortable **niche** for himself.

___ *Niche* means   A. a shared opinion.   B. a suitable place.   C. an education.

9 transcend
(trăn-sĕnd′)
-verb

- The psychic convinced her clients that she could **transcend** time and space and talk directly with the dead.
- Yoga can help one **transcend** the cares of the world and reach a state of relaxation.

___ *Transcend* means   A. to participate in.   B. to go past.   C. to use up.

10 waive
(wāv)
-verb

- The defendant decided to **waive** his right to an attorney and, instead, speak for himself in court.
- Since Lin had studied so much math on her own, the school **waived** the requirement that she take high school algebra.

___ *Waive* means   A. to lose.   B. to honor.   C. to give up.

Matching Words with Definitions

Following are definitions of the ten words. Clearly write or print each word next to its definition. The sentences above and on the previous page will help you decide on the meaning of each word.

1. _____ Not requiring special skills or higher intellectual abilities

2. _____ The ability to share in someone else's feelings or thoughts

3. _____ To rise above or go beyond the limits of; exceed

4. _____ To honor the memory of someone or something, as with a ceremony; celebrate; observe

5. _____ To willingly give up (as a claim, privilege, or right); do without

6. _____ An opinion held by everyone (or almost everyone) involved

7. _____ Self-satisfied; feeling too much satisfaction with oneself or one's accomplishments

8. _____ Steady, determined, and careful in work

9. _____ An activity or situation especially suited to a person

10. _____ To use up

CAUTION: Do not go any further until you are sure the above answers are correct. Then you can use the definitions to help you in the following practices. Your goal is eventually to know the words well enough so that you don't need to check the definitions at all.

Sentence Check 1

Using the answer line provided, complete each item below with the correct word from the box. Use each word once.

A. commemorate	B. complacent	C. consensus	D. deplete	E. diligent
F. empathy	G. menial	H. niche	I. transcend	J. waive

_____ 1. The hair salon got off to a good start, but then the owners became ___ about their success and stopped trying to attract new customers.

_____ 2. Many people believe that Shakespeare's works ___ those of all other authors.

_____ 3. My grandfather, who's recovering from heart surgery, is weak, so it doesn't take much effort for him to ___ the little energy he has.

_____ 4. The American Inventors' Association gathered at a banquet to ___ Thomas Edison.

_____ 5. The old man decided to ___ any claim he had to the family fortune, preferring to see the money go to the younger generation.

_____ 6. Dr. Grange is a brilliant mathematician, but she lacks ___ for her students. She doesn't understand how they can find some problems so difficult.

_____ 7. I had hoped the restaurant would be good, but our group's ___ was that the food was only so-so, and the service was even worse.

_____ 8. Arnie has been ___ in his study of German because he hopes to speak the language with his relatives from Germany when they visit next summer.

_____ 9. The children like to help out at the family restaurant, but they are able to perform only ___ tasks, such as mopping floors and cleaning tables.

_____ 10. Several sessions with a career counselor helped Suzanne consider what her ___ in the working world might be.

NOTE: Now check your answers to these items by turning to page 130. Going over the answers carefully will help you prepare for the next two practices, for which answers are not given.

Sentence Check 2

Using the answer lines provided, complete each item below with **two** words from the box. Use each word once.

_____niche_____
_____ 1–2. My mother could have stayed in her comfortable ___ as part of the secretarial pool, but she was averse° to remaining there. She wanted to ___ the limits of that job and become an executive herself.

_____consensus_____
_____empathy_____ 3–4. In high school, Julio was voted "Most Likely to Become a Psychologist." It was the ___ of his classmates that he was the student endowed° with the most ___ for other people.

_____waive_____
_____ 5–6. Lynn begged the bank to ___ the overdraft charge of thirty dollars, telling them that it would entirely ___ her savings.

_____   7–8. Dr. Roberts and Dr. Krill practice medicine very differently. Dr. Roberts
_____   is ___ about reading journals and learning new techniques. Conversely°,
Dr. Krill is more ___ and never tries anything new.

commerole   9–10. "On this, our hundredth anniversary celebration," said the company
diligent   president, "I'd like to ___ our founder with a toast. He ran the company from
top to bottom, doing even such ___ jobs as emptying garbage cans. He truly
exemplified° the values of dedication and hard work."

Final Check: *A Model Teacher*

Here is a final opportunity for you to strengthen your knowledge of the ten words. First read the following
selection carefully. Then fill in each blank with a word from the box at the top of the previous page.
(Context clues will help you figure out which word goes in which blank.) Use each word once.

At Eastman High School reunions, the conversation usually
gets around to the question "Who was our best teacher?"
And year after year, the (1)_____ of the
graduates has been that Mr. MacDonald was the best. Many
remember Joe MacDonald as the epitome° of teaching—the
teacher against whom they measured all others.

He had started his professional life as a highly paid
attorney. However, never at home with the law, he left his
lucrative° practice and found his (2)_____

© Monkey Business Images/shutterstock.com

as an English teacher in the shabby classrooms at Eastman. Mr. MacDonald somehow helped his students
(3)_____ their broken-down surroundings and experience the magic in the words
of Shakespeare, Dickinson, or Frost. Even those who tended to avoid reading began to think there might be
something to this literature stuff after all.

Mr. MacDonald's enthusiasm for his work was never (4)_____(e)d. In fact,
instead of being used up, his excitement actually increased through the years. Other teachers became
(5)_____ about their work and did only brief lesson preparation. But Mr. MacDonald
never became lazy; he was as (6)_____ as an eager first-year teacher. He could
often be found talking with students after school, as his great (7)_____ for
students—he had good rapport° with them and understood their problems—was well known. He was
fun, too. On the first really beautiful spring day of each year, he'd (8)_____ his lesson
plan and take the class outdoors to sit in the sunshine and talk about literature. And no task was too
(9)_____ for him. He was often seen picking up trash from the grounds—something
other teachers would never do.

After Mr. MacDonald's retirement, his former students wanted to honor him in some way. They
thought about a statue, but decided to (10)_____ his teaching in the way that he'd
like best, with a college scholarship for an Eastman student, which was established in his name.

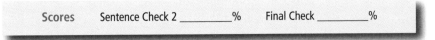

Scores   Sentence Check 2 _____%   Final Check _____%

Enter your scores above and in the **Vocabulary Performance Chart** on the inside back cover of the book.

The box at the right lists twenty-five words from Unit Three. Using the clues at the bottom of the page, fill in these words to complete the puzzle that follows.

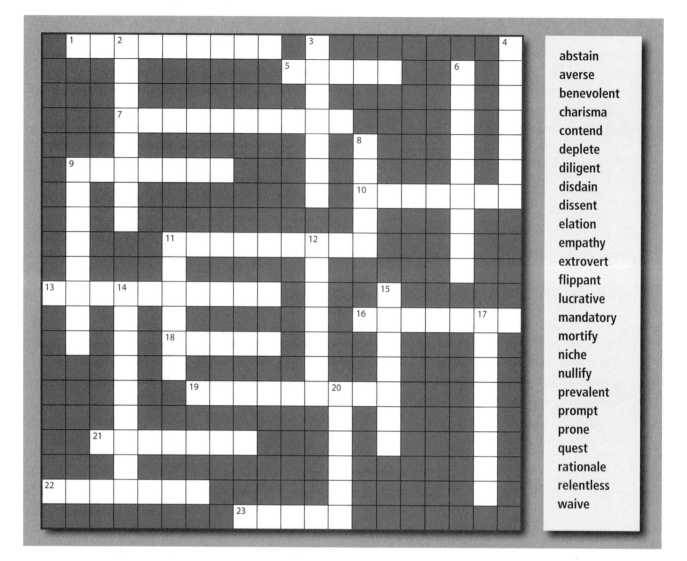

abstain
averse
benevolent
charisma
contend
deplete
diligent
disdain
dissent
elation
empathy
extrovert
flippant
lucrative
mandatory
mortify
niche
nullify
prevalent
prompt
prone
quest
rationale
relentless
waive

ACROSS

1. Profitable; well-paying
5. An activity or situation especially suited to a person
7. Persistent; continuous
9. An attitude or feeling of contempt; scorn
10. The ability to share in someone else's feelings or thoughts
11. Widespread; common
13. Charitable
16. To humiliate or embarrass
18. Having a tendency; inclined
19. The underlying reasons for something; logical basis
21. To use up
22. To hold oneself back from something; refrain
23. To willingly give up (as a claim, privilege, or right); do without

DOWN

2. The quality of a leader which captures great popular devotion; personal magnetism; charm
3. Disagreement
4. To make legally ineffective; cancel
6. Required
8. A search; pursuit
9. Steady, determined, and careful in work
11. To urge into action
12. A feeling of great joy or pride
14. An outgoing, sociable person
15. To state to be so; claim; affirm
17. Disrespectful and not serious enough
20. Having a feeling of dislike or distaste for something

PART A

Choose the word that best completes each item and write it in the space provided.

_____ 1. ___ to oversleeping, Rashid keeps his alarm clock across the room so he has to get out of bed to turn it off.

     A. Flippant   B. Lucrative   C. Prone   D. Mandatory

_____ 2. Alcohol is involved in nearly half of all traffic deaths in the United States, so people should ___ from drinking and driving.

     A. affiliate   B. abstain   C. contend   D. endow

_____ 3. When I realized that I didn't have enough money for holiday gifts, I decided to overcome the ___ by taking an extra part-time job in December.

     A. charisma   B. perception   C. dissent   D. deficit

_____ 4. Keith is an excellent mental-health counselor who feels genuine ___ for those who come to him for help.

     A. elation   B. quest   C. empathy   D. niche

_____ 5. Though pleased with the A on her last English paper, Lee was careful not to become ___—she began work on the next assignment immediately.

     A. complacent   B. traumatic   C. ominous   D. menial

_____ 6. My sister didn't find her career ___ until she took a computer coding class and discovered her talent for programming.

     A. proponent   B. niche   C. consensus   D. impasse

_____ 7. When Scott won the gymnastics competition, his parents' ___ was as great as his own joy and pride.

     A. elation   B. deficit   C. expulsion   D. charisma

_____ 8. ___ of gun control point out that gun accidents in American homes result in over a thousand deaths each year.

     A. Quests   B. Agnostics   C. Proponents   D. Extroverts

_____ 9. I'm not quick with home repairs, but I'm ___. I work steadily and carefully until I get the job done.

     A. diligent   B. complacent   C. flippant   D. ominous

_____ 10. The talks between the two countries reached a(n) ___ when each side claimed the oil-rich border area as its own.

     A. charisma   B. rapport   C. elation   D. impasse

(Continues on next page)

PART B

On the answer line, write the letter of the choice that best completes each item.

_____ 11. Joel seems to believe that his friends exist in order to serve him. **Conversely**, Julie
    A. believes she exists to serve her friends.   C. has far fewer friends than Joel.
    B. agrees with Joel's point of view.   D. is friends with Kori.

_____ 12. Napoleon Bonaparte was so **averse** to cats that he
    A. insisted one live in every room of his palace.   C. sneezed and itched whenever one was near.
    B. stroked one for luck every morning.   D. left the room in disgust if one entered.

_____ 13. Elaine works hard at her job as a lawyer. But for **diversion**, she
    A. reads all the latest law journals to keep up with recent developments.
    B. writes briefs, attends hearings, and meets with clients.
    C. gardens and plays field hockey.
    D. attended college and law school.

_____ 14. Knowing that her auto accident had been a **traumatic** experience, Beverly's friends
    A. expected her to heal soon.
    B. were hesitant to make her talk about the horrible event.
    C. wondered why she was making such a big deal of it.
    D. knew she would be joking about it soon.

_____ 15. A frequent dream of mine always **mortifies** me. In it,
    A. I am in public and suddenly realize I'm naked.
    B. I can fly as easily as a bird.
    C. I am in my childhood home talking with my father, who is young and healthy again.
    D. I am in a furious argument with a coworker whom I dislike.

_____ 16. If you **aspire** to be an Olympic swimmer,
    A. then find a sport you prefer.   C. become a coach instead.
    B. you must be ready to practice continually.   D. you may have a fear of water.

_____ 17. A child with **relentless** questions is probably
    A. ill.   C. curious.
    B. angry.   D. too shy to ask.

_____ 18. A person **endowed** with an honest nature
    A. wishes he had an honest nature.   C. pretends to have an honest nature.
    B. is lacking an honest nature.   D. possesses an honest nature.

_____ 19. **Ominous** music in a movie score generally means that
    A. a love scene is about to happen.   C. an exciting action scene is about to happen.
    B. something scary or evil is about to happen.   D. the opening credits are about to be shown.

_____ 20. The boss's **perception** of Cory was
    A. the comment "Good morning."   C. the afternoon shift.
    B. that Cory was a hard worker.   D. eight dollars an hour.

Score   (Number correct) _____ x 5 = _____ %

Enter your score above and in the **Vocabulary Performance Chart** on the inside back cover of the book.

PART A

Complete each item with a word from the box. Use each word once.

A. **commemorate**	B. **consensus**	C. **contend**	D. **divulge**	E. **extrovert**
F. **flippant**	G. **lucrative**	H. **poignant**	I. **prevalent**	J. **quest**
K. **rapport**	L. **rationale**	M. **reprisal**		

_____ 1. In some fairy tales, the hero searches far and wide, on a(n) ___ for some precious object or missing person.

_____ 2. When her brother kept taking her bike without asking, Meg's ___ was simply not to warn him that one of the tires was going flat.

_____ 3. The street's residents ___ that they complained for months about the huge pothole before the city government did anything about it.

_____ 4. I think it's selfish of Dolly not to ___ her secret recipe for coconut custard pie.

_____ 5. The ___ among the city's sportswriters is that Bridgewater High will win the basketball championship this year.

_____ 6. With violent crime so ___, some newspaper reporters now wear bulletproof vests when they cover a story.

_____ 7. When the principal asked Randy why he had spilled milk on some girls in the lunchroom, his ___ response was "Because they looked thirsty."

_____ 8. It was ___ to see the bear immediately adopt the orphaned cub.

_____ 9. I have excellent ___ with my brother, but I haven't spoken to my older sister for years.

_____ 10. On Presidents' Day, the nation ___s George Washington and Abraham Lincoln.

_____ 11. Rudy is such a(n) ___ that he makes friends with most of the customers at his beauty salon.

_____ 12. My ___ for using cloth napkins is that they result in fewer trees being cut down to make paper napkins.

_____ 13. Halloween is ___ for candy manufacturers. The holiday earns them about a billion dollars a year.

(Continues on next page)

PART B

Write **C** if the italicized word is used **correctly**. Write **I** if the word is used **incorrectly**.

_____ 14. After working in a hospital one summer, Andy has great *disdain* for the hard-working nurses he feels serve the patients so well.

_____ 15. The comedian Groucho Marx once joked that he wouldn't want to *affiliate* himself with any club that would accept him as a member.

_____ 16. By careful saving, I managed to *deplete* my bank account from $80 to almost $1,200 by the summer's end.

_____ 17. A course in American history isn't *mandatory* at most colleges, but our school does require first-year students to take one.

_____ 18. Halloween has *contemporary* roots. Each year, the ancient Irish would dress as demons and witches to frighten away ghosts who might otherwise claim their bodies.

_____ 19. In a democracy, it's important for people to *waive* their right to vote.

_____ 20. The *benevolent* boss laid workers off without even giving them a week's pay.

_____ 21. The TV contract will be *nullified* if the star misses any more rehearsals.

_____ 22. Whenever it snowed, the *congenial* boy next door would throw tightly packed snowballs at me.

_____ 23. "That bow tie *detracts* from Alan's appearance," said Paloma. "He looks strangled and gift-wrapped."

_____ 24. Wayne has *transcended* his usual good grades by failing three of his four classes this semester.

_____ 25. Because *menial* tasks require little thought, I was able to plan some of my essay while cleaning my apartment yesterday.

Score   (Number correct) _____ x 4 = _____%

PART A: Synonyms

In the space provided, write the letter of the choice that is most nearly the **same** in meaning as the **boldfaced** word.

____	1. **niche**	A. comfort	B. assignment	C. search	D. suitable place
____	2. **empathy**	A. understanding	B. great pride	C. anger	D. amusement
____	3. **ominous**	A. angry	B. criminal	C. threatening	D. not religious
____	4. **endow**	A. rise above	B. provide	C. lessen	D. have
____	5. **prompt**	A. discourage	B. conceal	C. agree	D. move to action
____	6. **rationale**	A. reasons	B. disagreement	C. great joy	D. limits
____	7. **nullify**	A. cancel	B. avoid	C. reveal	D. oppose
____	8. **perception**	A. desire	B. impression	C. knowledge	D. perfection
____	9. **diversion**	A. amusement	B. support	C. pride	D. division
____	10. **poignant**	A. friendly	B. dangerous	C. touching	D. required
____	11. **relentless**	A. unwilling	B. angry	C. constant	D. in an opposite way
____	12. **reprisal**	A. report	B. disagreement	C. surprise	D. revenge
____	13. **menial**	A. lowly	B. uncaring	C. uncommon	D. manly
____	14. **traumatic**	A. noisy	B. dramatic	C. advanced	D. emotionally painful
____	15. **charisma**	A. generosity	B. health	C. charm	D. knowledge
____	16. **transcend**	A. cancel	B. exceed	C. happen	D. respond
____	17. **aspire**	A. join	B. follow	C. succeed	D. desire
____	18. **prone**	A. tending	B. menacing	C. talented	D. legally allowed
____	19. **quest**	A. sympathy	B. hope	C. proper place	D. search
____	20. **lucrative**	A. agreeable	B. profitable	C. common	D. expensive
____	21. **diligent**	A. self-satisfied	B. hard-working	C. modern	D. unlikely
____	22. **rapport**	A. relationship	B. explanation	C. search	D. logical basis
____	23. **impasse**	A. disadvantage	B. lack	C. dead end	D. meantime
____	24. **abstain**	A. join	B. use up	C. do without	D. long for
____	25. **divulge**	A. tell	B. exaggerate	C. go beyond	D. disagree

(Continues on next page)

PART B: Antonyms

In the space provided, write the letter of the choice that is most nearly the **opposite** in meaning to the **boldfaced** word.

_____ 26. **congenial**   A. in doubt   B. far away   C. dissatisfied   D. disagreeable

_____ 27. **prevalent**   A. incorrect   B. difficult   C. uncommon   D. unpopular

_____ 28. **waive**   A. claim   B. forgive   C. go below   D. oppose

_____ 29. **mandatory**   A. unnecessary   B. easy   C. welcome   D. unlikely

_____ 30. **complacent**   A. different   B. self-doubting   C. uncomplicated   D. trustworthy

_____ 31. **proponent**   A. newcomer   B. inner-directed person   C. opponent   D. voter

_____ 32. **conversely**   A. expertly   B. boldly   C. late   D. in the same way

_____ 33. **flippant**   A. silent   B. persistent   C. curious   D. respectful

_____ 34. **affiliate**   A. agree   B. quit   C. recognize   D. join

_____ 35. **contend**   A. conclude   B. depend   C. deny   D. discontinue

_____ 36. **disdain**   A. good health   B. agreement   C. comfort   D. admiration

_____ 37. **mortify**   A. make proud   B. hide   C. disappoint   D. agree with

_____ 38. **commemorate**   A. recall   B. dishonor   C. discourage   D. praise

_____ 39. **elation**   A. illness   B. sadness   C. cruelty   D. escape

_____ 40. **deficit**   A. excess   B. correctness   C. support   D. work

_____ 41. **contemporary**   A. popular   B. antique   C. uncommon   D. unimproved

_____ 42. **deplete**   A. prefer   B. occur   C. lose   D. increase

_____ 43. **agnostic**   A. doubter of God   B. loner   C. believer in God   D. prophet

_____ 44. **benevolent**   A. cruel   B. unhappy   C. poor   D. conceited

_____ 45. **extrovert**   A. opponent   B. worker   C. leader   D. shy person

_____ 46. **averse**   A. effective   B. tending toward   C. doubting   D. done slowly

_____ 47. **dissent**   A. agreement   B. pleasure   C. success   D. prediction

_____ 48. **consensus**   A. full count   B. majority   C. impression   D. minority opinion

_____ 49. **detract**   A. conclude   B. remember   C. add to   D. face

_____ 50. **expulsion**   A. recognition   B. welcoming   C. payment   D. regret

Score   (Number correct) _____ x 2 = _____%

Enter your score above and in the **Vocabulary Performance Chart** on the inside back cover of the book.

Each item below starts with a pair of words in CAPITAL LETTERS. For each item, figure out the relationship between these two words. Then decide which of the choices (A, B, C, or D) expresses a similar relationship. Write the letter of your choice on the answer line.

_____ 1. POIGNANT : TRAGEDY ::
    A. mobile : motionless
    B. depressing : comedy
    C. giggle : baby
    D. noisy : riot

_____ 2. PROMPT : DISCOURAGE ::
    A. careful : careless
    B. book : library
    C. fragrant : flower
    D. late : tardy

_____ 3. FLIPPANT : REMARK ::
    A. runner : sprint
    B. insulting : gesture
    C. modest : humble
    D. singer : chorus

_____ 4. REPRISAL : ENEMY ::
    A. tears : joke
    B. cooperation : teammate
    C. revenge : ally
    D. terror : fear

_____ 5. DIVERSION : FISHING ::
    A. work : play
    B. fun : exciting
    C. guitar : drum
    D. dessert : apple pie

_____ 6. AGNOSTIC : RELIGIOUS ::
    A. salesperson : persuasive
    B. secretary : telephone
    C. hermit : sociable
    D. corn : crop

_____ 7. DISSENT : DISAGREEMENT ::
    A. remedy : solution
    B. chemist : scientist
    C. discord : harmony
    D. rival : helpful

_____ 8. DEFICIT : SURPLUS ::
    A. debt : poverty
    B. border : interior
    C. clouds : rain
    D. race car : speedy

_____ 9. CONTEMPORARY : OLD-FASHIONED ::
    A. outdated : old
    B. copy : original
    C. thoughtful : gift
    D. handlebar : bicycle

_____ 10. EXTROVERT : FRIENDLINESS ::
    A. performer : shyness
    B. victor : defeated
    C. artist : creativity
    D. clown : circus

(Continues on next page)

_____ 11. COMMEMORATE : ANNIVERSARY ::
      A. trophy : winner   C. break : diamond
      B. horn : bull   D. regret : mistake

_____ 12. DILIGENT : HARD-WORKING ::
      A. presence : absence   C. frightful : comforting
      B. dirty : unclean   D. silk : torn

_____ 13. EXPULSION : SCHOOL ::
      A. eviction : apartment   C. celebration : funeral
      B. graduation : college   D. exercise : gym

_____ 14. COMPLACENT : SELF-DOUBT ::
      A. tired : exhaustion   C. transparent : clearness
      B. uninterested : indifference   D. rigid : flexibility

_____ 15. NICHE : SUITABLE ::
      A. kitchen cabinet : cereal   C. haunted house : scary
      B. high school : classroom   D. doctor's office : chilly

_____ 16. CHARISMA : BLAND ::
      A. honest : trustworthy   C. premature : early
      B. modesty : boastful   D. emergency : rush

_____ 17. IMPASSE : PROBLEMATIC ::
      A. round : corners   C. alien : native
      B. success : satisfying   D. traitor : betrayal

_____ 18. DETRACT : IMPROVE ::
      A. blame : error   C. criticize : scold
      B. open : door   D. ascend : descend

_____ 19. ELATION : WONDERFUL NEWS ::
      A. pain : injury   C. satisfaction : failure
      B. wisdom : ignorance   D. football : sport

_____ 20. OMINOUS : STORM CLOUDS ::
      A. bright : fog   C. flock : seagull
      B. fragrant : flowers   D. sophomore : grade

Score   (Number correct) _____ x 5 = _____ %

Enter your score above and in the **Vocabulary Performance Chart** on the inside back cover of the book.

Unit Four

Chapter 16

condone	furtive
contemplate	gape
feasible	pathetic
feign	precedent
fiscal	punitive

Chapter 17

cryptic	inhibition
deficient	ironic
depict	rupture
detrimental	saturate
implicit	vindictive

Chapter 18

constrict	habitat
exhaustive	pragmatic
fallible	pretentious
formulate	reconcile
genial	vile

Chapter 19

avid	mediate
dwindle	muted
esteem	nurture
evoke	pacify
legacy	transient

Chapter 20

aloof	longevity
ambivalent	magnitude
augment	mundane
dispel	obscure
explicit	render

condone	furtive
contemplate	gape
feasible	pathetic
feign	precedent
fiscal	punitive

Ten Words in Context

In the space provided, write the letter of the meaning closest to that of each **boldfaced** word. Use the context of the sentences to help you figure out each word's meaning.

1 condone
(kən-dōn')
-verb

● I cannot **condone** Elaine's smoking in public. It threatens other people's health.

● Teachers may overlook it when you're three minutes late. But they are not going to **condone** your walking into class a half hour late.

___ *Condone* means   A. to excuse.   B. to recall.   C. to punish.

2 contemplate
(kŏn'təm-plāt')
-verb

● Because Ben hadn't studied for the test, he **contemplated** cheating. He quickly realized, however, that the eagle-eyed teacher would spot him.

● We **contemplated** getting a dog but realized that we travel too often to be good pet owners.

___ *Contemplate* means   A. to consider.   B. to pretend.   C. to avoid.

3 feasible
(fē'zə-bəl)
-adjective

● It isn't **feasible** for me to work full time and keep the house clean unless someone helps me with the cleaning chores.

● Maya told her supervisor, "It just isn't **feasible** for this staff to do the work of the two people who were fired. You need to hire more people."

___ *Feasible* means   A. wrong.   B. legal.   C. possible.

4 feign
(fān)
-verb

● Since I had heard about my surprise party, I had to **feign** shock when everyone yelled, "Surprise!"

● You can **feign** a head cold by pretending you're too stuffed up to pronounce an *l, n,* or *m.* Try it by saying, "I have a code id by dose."

___ *Feign* means   A. to wish for.   B. to prove.   C. to fake.

5 fiscal
(fĭs'kəl)
-adjective

● The gift shop closed because of **fiscal** problems. It simply didn't make enough money to cover its expenses.

● Some states have passed laws allowing child-support payments to be taken directly from the paychecks of divorced parents who ignore their **fiscal** responsibility to their children.

___ *Fiscal* means   A. emotional.   B. financial.   C. unfair.

6 furtive
(fûr'tĭv)
-adjective

● At the football game, a guard in the stands noticed the **furtive** movement of a thief's hand toward a spectator's pocket.

● Students cheated on the exam by sending **furtive** messages on their smartphones to share their answers.

___ *Furtive* means   A. sneaky.   B. dependable.   C. serious.

inaugurato

7 gape
(gāp)
-verb

● Everyone stopped to **gape** at the odd-looking sculpture in front of the library.
● Because drivers slowed down to **gape** at an accident in the southbound lanes, northbound traffic was backed up for miles.

__ *Gape* means   A. to yell.   B. to appreciate.   C. to stare.

8 pathetic
(pə-thĕt′ĭk)
-adjective

● That plumber's work was **pathetic**. Not only does the faucet still drip, but now the pipe is leaking.
● Health care in some areas of the world is **pathetic**. People are dying of diseases that are easily treatable with modern medicine.

__ *Pathetic* means   A. ordinary.   B. miserable.   C. expensive.

9 precedent
(prĕs′ĭ-dĕnt)
-noun

● When Jean's employer gave her three months off after her baby was born, a **precedent** was set for anyone else in the company who became a parent.
● To set a **precedent**, the teacher gave the student who stole the exam an F for the entire course. "Others will think twice before they do the same," he explained.

__ *Precedent* means   A. a question.   B. a delay.   C. a model.

10 punitive
(pyōō′nĭ-tĭv)
-adjective

● Judge Starn is especially **punitive** with drunken drivers, giving every one of them a jail term.
● Many parents find that reward is a better basis for teaching children than **punitive** action is.

__ *Punitive* means   A. punishing.   B. forgiving.   C. uneven.

Matching Words with Definitions

Following are definitions of the ten words. Clearly write or print each word next to its definition. The sentences above and on the previous page will help you decide on the meaning of each word.

1. _____ Possible; able to be done

2. _____ Done or behaving so as not to be noticed; secret

3. _____ To stare in wonder or amazement, often with one's mouth wide open

4. _____ Anything that may serve as an example in dealing with later similar circumstances

5. _____ To forgive or overlook

6. _____ Giving or involving punishment; punishing

7. _____ Financial

8. _____ To think about seriously

9. _____ Pitifully inadequate or unsuccessful

10. _____ To pretend; give a false show of

CAUTION: Do not go any further until you are sure the above answers are correct. Then you can use the definitions to help you in the following practices. Your goal is eventually to know the words well enough so that you don't need to check the definitions at all.

Sentence Check 1

Using the answer line provided, complete each item below with the correct word from the box. Use each word once.

A. **condone**	B. **contemplate**	C. **feasible**	D. **feign**	E. **fiscal**
F. **furtive**	G. **gape**	H. **pathetic**	I. **precedent**	J. **punitive**

_____ 1. The coach does not ___ fighting. He believes that every problem has a nonviolent solution.

_____ 2. It's not ___ for me to attend two weddings in the same afternoon, so I'll have to choose between them.

_____ 3. Lawyers can strengthen a case by finding a useful ___ among previous similar cases.

_____ 4. From time to time, I ___ attending business school, but so far I've made no firm decision.

_____ 5. Disabled people don't like others to ___ at them. Instead of a stare, a simple smile would be appreciated.

_____ 6. My mother wasn't usually ___, but one day I pushed her too far, and she said, "If you do that one more time, I will send you to your room for the rest of your adolescence."

_____ 7. When I gave my oral report in class, I tried to ___ confidence, but my shaking legs revealed my nervousness.

_____ 8. Mr. Hall's living conditions were ___. There was no heat or electricity in his apartment, and the walls were crumbling.

_____ 9. The people on the elevator didn't want to stare at the patch on my eye, but several took ___ glances.

_____ 10. Giving children an allowance can help them learn about ___ planning; if they want to purchase something, they must save up for it.

NOTE: Now check your answers to these items by turning to page 130. Going over the answers carefully will help you prepare for the next two practices, for which answers are not given.

Sentence Check 2

Using the answer lines provided, complete each item below with **two** words from the box. Use each word once.

_____punitive_____
_____contemplate_____   1–2. Some parents take only ___ measures when children misbehave. They never take time to ___ the benefits of a gentler approach. However, encouragement is often more effective than punishment.

_____feasible_____
_____fiscal_____   3–4. "Would it be ___ for us to buy a new copy machine?" Hal asked at the office budget meeting. The boss replied, "Unfortunately, our ___ situation is too tight. That purchase would deplete° our funds and create a deficit° in our budget."

_____   5–6.   The ___ was set many years ago: When the winner of a beauty contest is
_____   announced, the runner-up ___s happiness for the winner, despite the fact that
                                   she is the opposite of happy at the moment.

__*contempore*_____   7–8.   The fourth-grade teacher said, "I will not ___ any ___ behavior in my class.
_____   Rita, please stop passing notes under your desk to Ellen."

_____   9–10.   Several passersby stopped to ___ at the homeless man and his ___ shelter,
_____   made of cardboard and a torn blanket. The heartbreaking sight moved one
                                   woman to go to a restaurant and buy a meal for the man.

Final Check: *Shoplifter*

Here is a final opportunity for you to strengthen your knowledge of the ten words. First read the following selection carefully. Then fill in each blank with a word from the box at the top of the previous page. (Context clues will help you figure out which word goes in which blank.) Use each word once.

Valerie took a (1)_____ glance around her. When it seemed that no one was watching, she stuffed a blue shirt into the bottom of her purse and darted out of the women's department. She walked slowly around the shoe department for a while and then left the store.

"Stop! You! Stop!" shouted a guard, who seemed to appear from nowhere. Then another man in street clothes grabbed her purse and pulled out the shirt.

"But . . . but . . . it's not mine. I don't know how it got there," Valerie cried.

The two men just looked at each other and laughed at the blatant° lie. The guard said, "That's what all shoplifters say. People steal without taking time to (2)_____ the possible results. Then when they're caught, they loudly (3)_____ innocence."

© SpeedKingz/shutterstock.com

As the guard began to phone the police, Valerie begged the men, "Please don't press charges. Please. This is the first time I've ever done anything like this, and I'll never do it again."

The men laughed again. "Your argument is (4)_____," the man in street clothes sneered°. "It's everyone's first time. Our store has a policy on shoplifters: It's mandatory° for us to press charges, even if it's the first offense. We can't set a bad (5)_____ by letting a shoplifter go, as if we (6)_____(e)d such crimes."

"That's right," said the guard. "Shoplifting is all too prevalent° in our store. This shirt costs only twenty dollars, but the twenties add up. Our (7)_____ officer reported a loss of about $150,000 worth of merchandise to shoplifters last year. So it simply isn't (8)_____ to let you walk away. Unfortunately, we have no choice but to take (9)_____ action."

Soon Valerie was led to the police car. She covered her face as other shoppers stopped to (10)_____ at the lovely young woman, an unlikely-looking criminal.

Scores	Sentence Check 2 _____%	Final Check _____%

Enter your scores above and in the **Vocabulary Performance Chart** on the inside back cover of the book.

cryptic	inhibition
deficient	ironic
depict	rupture
detrimental	saturate
implicit	vindictive

Ten Words in Context

In the space provided, write the letter of the meaning closest to that of each **boldfaced** word. Use the context of the sentences to help you figure out each word's meaning.

misterios

1 cryptic
(krĭp′tĭk)
-adjective

● Whenever I ask Tomas what's happening in his life, he always gives the same **cryptic** reply: "It's a green world, my friend."

● Next to the broken window was a **cryptic** note that said, "It was time."

__ *Cryptic* means   A. cruel.   B. puzzling.   C. humorous.

2 deficient
(dĭ-fĭsh′ənt)
-adjective

● When people have too little iron in their blood, it sometimes means that their diet is also **deficient** in iron.

● Gil's manners are **deficient**. For example, I've never heard him thank anyone for anything.

__ *Deficient* means   A. lacking.   B. sensitive.   C. increasing.

3 depict
(dĭ-pĭkt′)
-verb

● The painting **depicts** a typical nineteenth-century summer day in the park.

● Harriet Beecher Stowe's novel *Uncle Tom's Cabin* **depicted** the cruelty of slavery so forcefully that the book helped to begin the Civil War.

__ *Depict* means   A. to hide.   B. to show.   C. to predict.

perjudical

4 detrimental
(dĕ′trə-mĕn′təl)
-adjective

● Do you think all television is **detrimental** to children, or are some programs a positive influence on them?

● The gases from automobiles and factories have been so **detrimental** to the environment that some of the damage may be permanent.

__ *Detrimental* means   A. useful.   B. new.   C. damaging.

5 implicit
(ĭm-plĭs′ĭt)
-adjective

● When the gangster growled, "I'm sure you want your family to stay healthy," Harris understood the **implicit** threat.

● Although it's never been said, there's an **implicit** understanding that Carla will be promoted when Earl finally retires.

__ *Implicit* means   A. playful.   B. modern.   C. unspoken.

discrecion

6 inhibition
(ĭn′hə-bĭsh′ən)
-noun

● A two-year-old has no **inhibitions** about running around naked.

● Sarah's family is openly affectionate, with no **inhibitions** about hugging or kissing in public.

__ *Inhibition* means   A. an inner block.   B. a habit.   C. a purpose.

7 ironic
(ī-rŏn′ĭk)
-adjective

● It's **ironic** that Loretta is such a strict mother, because she was certainly wild in her youth.

● "The Gift of the Magi" is a short story with an **ironic** twist: A woman sells her long hair to buy a chain for her husband's watch, while her husband sells his watch to buy ornaments for her hair.

___ *Ironic* means   A. unexpected.   B. inadequate.   C. reasonable.

8 rupture
(rŭp′chər)
-verb

● If the dam were to **rupture**, the town would disappear under many feet of water.

● The bulge in the football player's stomach was caused by a muscle wall that had **ruptured** and would have to be repaired.

___ *Rupture* means   A. to heal.   B. to exist.   C. to come apart.

9 saturate
(săch′ə-rāt′)
-verb

● Most people like their cereal crunchy, but Teresa lets hers sit until the milk has **saturated** every piece.

● Studying history for three hours **saturated** my brain—I couldn't have absorbed one more bit of information.

___ *Saturate* means   A. to protect.   B. to empty.   C. to fill.

10 vindictive
(vĭn-dĭk′tĭv)
-adjective

● My grandmother isn't usually **vindictive**, but when her neighbor started throwing cigarette butts in her yard, she gathered and dumped them into his pool.

● After she was given two weeks' notice, the **vindictive** employee intentionally infected all the office computers with a virus.

___ *Vindictive* means   A. sympathetic.   B. spiteful.   C. puzzling.

Matching Words with Definitions

Following are definitions of the ten words. Clearly write or print each word next to its definition. The sentences above and on the previous page will help you decide on the meaning of each word.

1. _____ A holding back or blocking of some action, feeling, or thought

2. _____ Having a vague or hidden meaning; mysterious

3. _____ Suggested but not directly expressed; unstated, but able to be understood

4. _____ Inclined to seek revenge; vengeful

5. _____ To represent in pictures or words; describe

6. _____ To burst or break apart

7. _____ Lacking something essential; inadequate; insufficient

8. _____ To soak or fill as much as possible

9. _____ Harmful; causing damage

10. _____ Opposite to what might be expected

CAUTION: Do not go any further until you are sure the above answers are correct. Then you can use the definitions to help you in the following practices. Your goal is eventually to know the words well enough so that you don't need to check the definitions at all.

Sentence Check 1

Using the answer line provided, complete each item below with the correct word from the box. Use each word once.

A. cryptic	B. deficient	C. depict	D. detrimental	E. implicit
F. inhibition	G. ironic	H. rupture	I. saturate	J. vindictive

_____ 1. Becky's usual lack of ___ was evident the day she came to class barefoot.

_____ 2. Even something as healthful as vitamins can be ___ to your health when taken in very large amounts.

_____ 3. Isn't it ___ that the richest man in town won the million-dollar lottery?

_____ 4. When the pressure in the gas pipe became too great, the pipe ___(e)d.

_____ 5. A person can be intelligent and yet be ___ in common sense.

_____ 6. Although it's not written in teachers' contracts, there is a(n) ___ understanding that teachers will spend time preparing lessons and grading students' work.

_____ 7. The aroma of Gretchen's perfume so ___(e)d the air in the car that Steve coughed and rolled down a window.

_____ 8. The fifth-grade assignment was written in riddles. Everyone laughed as the students tried to make out the teacher's ___ message.

_____ 9. The clans, or families, of ancient Scotland were extremely ___. If anyone from another clan harmed one of their members, the others would take full revenge.

_____ 10. In the novel *Oliver Twist*, Charles Dickens ___s life in an English orphanage as truly pathetic°, with little food and no love.

NOTE: Now check your answers to these items by turning to page 130. Going over the answers carefully will help you prepare for the next two practices, for which answers are not given.

Sentence Check 2

Using the answer lines provided, complete each item below with **two** words from the box. Use each word once.

_____
_____ 1–2. I feel it's a waste of energy to retaliate° when someone has injured me, but my sister is always trying to get even with people. Her ___ attitude is ___ to her relationships with family and friends.

_____
_____ 3–4. Most viewers find the painting, with its dozens of dots on a white background, to be ___. However, it's possible to figure out what the painting ___s by mentally connecting the dots.

_____ 5–6. Water-balloon fights are fun until a balloon ___s against your clothes, and they get ___(e)d with cold water.

_____   7–8. Gerry feels people should "lose their ___s" and do whatever they feel like doing, but I think people who are totally ___ in self-control have poor manners.

_____   9–10. It's ___ that the book *Live Simply on Little Money* has made the author wealthy, since a(n) ___ message of the book is that the author himself requires little money.

Final Check: *Coffee Shop Blues*

Here is a final opportunity for you to strengthen your knowledge of the ten words. First read the following selection carefully. Then fill in each blank with a word from the box at the top of the previous page. (Context clues will help you figure out which word goes in which blank.) Use each word once.

It's (1)_____ that I work in a coffee shop, because I am (2)_____ in a love for coffee—in fact, I can't stand it. When I saw the "Help Wanted" sign in the shop window, I worried that my negative feelings about coffee would be a problem. But I really needed the job, so I got over my (3)_____s and applied.

Fortunately, my position involves taking orders and making drinks—not drinking them—so my dislike of coffee is not (4)_____ to my doing a good job. Of course, I did have to learn the vocabulary of the coffee shop. During my first days, an order such as a "nonfat one-pump no-whip mocha" did seem (5)_____, but I eventually caught on.

I also had trouble early on learning how to work in such a small space. During the morning rush, it was hard to avoid bumping into my coworkers behind the counter. I still recall with embarrassment the time I crashed hard into Pablo. The cup of iced coffee I was holding (6)_____(e)d, and the drink (7)_____(e)d his entire uniform.

While handling orders is no longer a challenge, some customers can be. I certainly don't mean to (8)_____ all my customers as unpleasant; most of them are nice, and we have good rapport°. But this is my theory: the more complicated the order, the more annoying the person. When someone asks for an "iced half-caf cinnamon soy skinny latte," the (9)_____ message seems to be, "I am an extremely self-important and snobby person who is impossible to please." I smile and take the order but imagine doing something (10)_____ like "accidentally" spilling a bit of the drink on their lap. But that would be wrong—satisfying, but wrong.

Scores   Sentence Check 2 _____%   Final Check _____%

Enter your scores above and in the **Vocabulary Performance Chart** on the inside back cover of the book.

constrict	habitat
exhaustive	pragmatic
fallible	pretentious
formulate	reconcile
genial	vile

Ten Words in Context

In the space provided, write the letter of the meaning closest to that of each **boldfaced** word. Use the context of the sentences to help you figure out each word's meaning.

(handwritten) Constrict

1 constrict
(kən-strĭkt′)
-*verb*

● The summer highway construction will **constrict** traffic by confining it to only two lanes.

● For centuries in China, girls' feet were **constricted** with binding to keep them from growing to normal size. Women's feet were considered most attractive if they were less than four inches long.

__ *Constrict* means   A. to expand.   B. to repair.   C. to squeeze.

2 exhaustive
(ĭg-zô′stĭv)
-*adjective*

● Don't buy a used car without putting it through an **exhaustive** inspection. Check every detail, from hood to trunk.

● My history teacher recommended an **exhaustive** thousand-page biography of Alexander Hamilton, but who has time to read such a thorough account?

__ *Exhaustive* means   A. smooth.   B. detailed.   C. narrow.

3 fallible
(făl′ə-bəl)
-*adjective*

● "I know we all are **fallible**," the boss told his workers. "But do you have to make so many of your mistakes on company time?"

● When they are little, kids think their parents can do no wrong; but when they become teenagers, their parents suddenly seem **fallible**.

__ *Fallible* means   A. optimistic.   B. friendly.   C. imperfect.

4 formulate
(fôr′myə-lāt′)
-*verb*

● The author first **formulated** an outline of his plot and then began writing his mystery.

● Before stepping into his boss's office, Toshio had carefully **formulated** his case for a raise.

__ *Formulate* means   A. to develop.   B. to question.   C. to accept.

5 genial
(jēn′yəl)
-*adjective*

● I was worried that my grandmother's treatment at the nursing home might be harsh, so I was relieved when the nurses and aides turned out to be very **genial**.

● Stacey found her first dance instructor so rude and unpleasant that she changed to a more **genial** one.

__ *Genial* means   A. good-looking.   B. practical.   C. good-natured.

6 habitat
(hăb′ĭ-tăt)
-*noun*

● Many people believe that wild animals should be allowed to remain in their natural **habitats** and not be captured and put in zoos.

● Mosses can live in a large variety of humid **habitats**, from very cold to very hot.

__ *Habitat* means   A. a pattern.   B. a plan.   C. a territory.

106

7 pragmatic
(prăg-măt′ĭk)
-*adjective*

- We always called my sister "Practical Polly" because she was the most **pragmatic** member of the family.
- When Vince was single, he spent most of his money on travel. Now that he has a family to support, he must spend his money in more **pragmatic** ways.

___ *Pragmatic* means   A. sensible.   B. patient.   C. pleasant.

8 pretentious
(prē-těn′shəs)
-*adjective*
arrogant

- Dana's classmates don't like her because she's so **pretentious**. It's hard to like someone who acts as if she knows it all.
- My aunt marked her husband's grave with a large, **pretentious** monument, as though he were a member of a royal family.

___ *Pretentious* means   A. overly imaginative.   B. important-seeming.   C. cruel.

9 reconcile
(rěk′ən-sīl′)
-*verb*

- When my grandfather died, we worked hard to **reconcile** Grandma to the fact that he was really gone.
- After his third wreck in six months, Ahmed **reconciled** himself to living somewhere along a bus line and doing without a car.

___ *Reconcile to* means   A. to bring to accept.   B. to frighten about.   C. to hide from.

10 vile
(vīl)
-*adjective*

- My sister loves a certain cheese that has the **vile** odor of something that fell off a garbage truck.
- When I finally get around to cleaning out the refrigerator, I always find some **vile** moldy leftovers at the back of a shelf.

___ *Vile* means   A. threatening.   B. natural.   C. nasty.

Matching Words with Definitions

Following are definitions of the ten words. Clearly write or print each word next to its definition. The sentences above and on the previous page will help you decide on the meaning of each word.

1. _____ To bring (oneself or someone else) to accept

2. _____ The natural environment of an animal or a plant

3. _____ Making a show of excellence or importance, especially when undeserved

4. _____ Capable of making an error

5. _____ To make smaller or narrower, as by squeezing or shrinking

6. _____ Covering all possible details; complete; thorough

7. _____ Friendly, pleasant, and kindly

8. _____ Offensive to the senses, feelings, or thoughts; disgusting

9. _____ To plan or express in an orderly way

10. _____ Practical

CAUTION: Do not go any further until you are sure the above answers are correct. Then you can use the definitions to help you in the following practices. Your goal is eventually to know the words well enough so that you don't need to check the definitions at all.

Sentence Check 1

Using the answer line provided, complete each item below with the correct word from the box. Use each word once.

A. constrict	B. exhaustive	C. fallible	D. formulate	E. genial
F. habitat	G. pragmatic	H. pretentious	I. reconcile	J. vile

_____ 1. My supervisor told me that if I wished to work on an independent project, I should first ___ a detailed plan of my idea.

_____ 2. Bright light ___s the pupils of our eyes, letting in less light. Darkness makes them wider, letting in more light.

_____ 3. My mother was forced to ___ herself to my independence when I moved into my own apartment.

_____ 4. Why is Debra acting so unfriendly today? She's usually so ___.

_____ 5. Our local diner serves the world's most ___ beef stew, full of big globs of fat.

_____ 6. When the auto mechanic said, "Well, I'm ___ like everyone else," I responded, "Yes, but your mistake almost got me flattened by a truck."

_____ 7. "It would be more ___," my brother said, "if you went to the grocery once a week for a larger order rather than going daily for just a few items."

_____ 8. Children's stories sometimes mistakenly show penguins at the North Pole. The birds' ___ is actually near the South Pole.

_____ 9. ___ about his intelligence, Norm tries to impress people by using big words.

_____ 10. For her term paper on orchids, Giselle did ___ research, covering every aspect of the flower's growth and marketing.

NOTE: Now check your answers to these items by turning to page 130. Going over the answers carefully will help you prepare for the next two practices, for which answers are not given.

Sentence Check 2

Using the answer lines provided, complete each item below with **two** words from the box. Use each word once.

_____
_____ 1–2. My uncle was not at all ___ about fiscal° matters. He would spend household money on lottery tickets and ___-smelling cigars and leave the family without any extra cash.

_____
_____ 3–4. Wildlife experts ___(e)d a plan to preserve what little remains of the gorilla's natural ___. Continued loss of that territory will threaten these magnificent animals and could even result in their extinction.

_____
_____ 5–6. "You want me to be perfect, but that's impossible!" I cried. "___ yourself to the fact that every one of us is ___." It wasn't until then that my mother realized how detrimental° her criticism had been to our relationship.

_____   7–8. At the sales seminar, employees were taught to be ___ with customers and
_____   never to seem ___, no matter how much they knew. Customers like warm,
                                    amiable° salespeople, not ones who show off.

_____   9–10. When our pet python escaped, we quickly made a(n) ___ search throughout
_____   the house and grounds. We found him wrapped around our dog, about to ___
                                    the poor mutt to death.

Final Check: *Roughing It*

Here is a final opportunity for you to strengthen your knowledge of the ten words. First read the following selection carefully. Then fill in each blank with a word from the box at the top of the previous page. (Context clues will help you figure out which word goes in which blank.) Use each word once.

"Whose brilliant idea was this, anyway?" Sara asked. "If people were intended to sleep on the ground and cook over a fire, we wouldn't have beds and microwave ovens."

"Stop complaining," Emily said. "At least *you've* got on dry clothes. You didn't end up walking through some (1)_____ mud because your canoe overturned. And you didn't have a(n) (2)_____ partner who claimed to know everything about canoeing but actually didn't know enough to steer around a rock."

© bokan/shutterstock.com

"So I made a mistake," George said. "We're all (3)_____."

"Well," Emily responded, "your mistake has lost us our tent. And our sleeping bags and clothes are saturated° with muddy water."

Then Doug spoke up. "It's no big deal. We didn't plan for this, so let's improvise. Sara and I will lend you clothes, and you two can squeeze into our tent."

"Squeeze is right, " said Emily. "Four in one tent won't work—it just isn't feasible°. We'll be so (4)_____(e)d that we won't be able to exhale."

"It's your choice," said Doug. "Decide if you want to be in a crowded tent or sleep out in this wild-animal (5)_____."

Sara couldn't resist adding, "If you had just listened to me this time and had been a bit more (6)_____ when planning for this trip, we wouldn't be in such a mess. You would have written a(n) (7)_____ list of what we would need, from A to Z. Then you would have (8)_____(e)d a clear plan for who would take what. Then we wouldn't be out here with two corkscrews but no plastic to wrap our belongings in."

"Let's just stop complaining before this degenerates° into a shouting match. Instead, let's try to be a little more (9)_____ with one another," said Doug. "Right now, we need to (10)_____ ourselves to our imperfect situation and not let it detract° so much from our vacation that we forget to have a good time."

| Scores | Sentence Check 2 _____% | Final Check _____% |

Enter your scores above and in the **Vocabulary Performance Chart** on the inside back cover of the book.

CHAPTER 19

avid	mediate
dwindle	muted
esteem	nurture
evoke	pacify
legacy	transient

Ten Words in Context

In the space provided, write the letter of the meaning closest to that of each **boldfaced** word. Use the context of the sentences to help you figure out each word's meaning.

dedicado

1 avid
(ăv′ĭd)
-*adjective*

● Suki, an **avid** reader, enjoys nothing more than a good science-fiction novel.
● Artie is such an **avid** sports fan that he has two televisions tuned to different sporting events so he doesn't miss any action.

___ *Avid* means   A. likable.   B. devoted.   C. helpful.

2 dwindle
(dwĭn′dəl)
-*verb*

● As the number of leaves on the tree **dwindled**, the number on the ground increased.
● By episode five in the TV show's first season, my interest began to **dwindle**. I never did watch the last episodes.

___ *Dwindle* means   A. to make sense.   B. to drop suddenly.   C. to decrease.

3 esteem
(ĕ-stēm′)
-*noun*

● When Mr. Bauer retired after coaching basketball for thirty years, his admiring students gave him a gold whistle as a sign of their **esteem**.
● The critics had such **esteem** for the play that they voted it "Best Drama of the Year."

___ *Esteem* means   A. concern.   B. admiration.   C. curiosity.

sacar

4 evoke
(ē-vōk′)
-*verb*

● Music can **evoke** powerful feelings. A sweet violin solo often moves its listeners to tears.
● The smells of cider and pumpkin pie **evoke** thoughts of autumn.

___ *Evoke* means   A. to bring out.   B. to shelter.   C. to follow.

legado

5 legacy
(lĕg′ə-sē)
-*noun*

● Ana's great-grandfather, grandmother, and mother were all musicians. She must have inherited their **legacy** of musical talent because she's an excellent piano and guitar player.
● One of the richest **legacies** that my mother handed down to me is the love of nature. I've inherited her interests in growing flowers and in hiking.

___ *Legacy* means   A. a memory.   B. a high hope.   C. an inherited gift.

resolver

6 mediate
(mē′dē-āt′)
-*verb*

● My father refused to **mediate** quarrels between my sister and me. He would say, "Settle your own fights."
● Each of the farmers claimed the stream was part of his property. Finally, they agreed to let the town council **mediate** their conflict.

___ *Mediate* means   A. to avoid.   B. to settle.   C. to observe.

7 muted
(myo͞o′təd)
-*adjective*

● When I put in my earplugs, the yelling from the next apartment becomes **muted** enough so that it no longer disturbs me.

● The artist used **muted** rather than bright colors, giving the painting a quiet, peaceful tone.

__ *Muted* means   A. soft.   B. temporary.   C. boring.

8 nurture
(nûr′chər)
-*verb*

● Although I often forget to water or feed my plants, my sister carefully **nurtures** her many ferns and violets.

● Many animals feed and protect their babies, but female fish, in general, do not **nurture** their young. The female only lays the eggs, which are guarded by the male until they hatch.

__ *Nurture* means   A. to inspect.   B. to seek out.   C. to care for.

9 pacify
(păs′ə-fī′)
-*verb*

● When I'm feeling nervous or upset, I often **pacify** myself with a soothing cup of mint tea.

● Not only did I anger Roberta by calling her boyfriend "a creep," but I failed to **pacify** her with my note of apology: "I'm sorry I called Mel a creep. It's not always wise to tell the truth."

__ *Pacify* means   A. to amuse.   B. to encourage.   C. to soothe.

10 transient
(trăn′shənt)
-*adjective*

● The drug's dangers include both permanent brain damage and **transient** side effects, such as temporarily blurred vision.

● Julia wants a lasting relationship, but Rico seems interested in only a **transient** one.

__ *Transient* means   A. dull.   B. short-lived.   C. hard to notice.

Matching Words with Definitions

Following are definitions of the ten words. Clearly write or print each word next to its definition. The sentences above and on the previous page will help you decide on the meaning of each word.

1. _____   Softened; toned down; made less intense

2. _____   Temporary; passing soon or quickly

3. _____   Enthusiastic, devoted; eager

4. _____   To make calm or peaceful

5. _____   To draw forth, as a mental image or a feeling

6. _____   To gradually lessen or shrink

7. _____   To settle (a conflict) by acting as a go-between

8. _____   High regard; respect; favorable opinion

9. _____   To promote development by providing nourishment, support, and protection

10. _____   Something handed down from people who have come before

CAUTION: Do not go any further until you are sure the above answers are correct. Then you can use the definitions to help you in the following practices. Your goal is eventually to know the words well enough so that you don't need to check the definitions at all.

Sentence Check 1

Using the answer line provided, complete each item below with the correct word from the box. Use each word once.

A. **avid**	B. **dwindle**	C. **esteem**	D. **evoke**	E. **legacy**
F. **mediate**	G. **muted**	H. **nurture**	I. **pacify**	J. **transient**

_____ 1. You must ___ a child with love and respect as well as with food and shelter.

_____ 2. At the party, Cara and I kept our conversation ___ so that no one would overhear us.

_____ 3. If you study too long at one sitting, your concentration will eventually begin to ___.

_____ 4. The photos in my album ___ many fond memories of my high-school friends.

_____ 5. When my newborn nephew starts to scream, his parents ___ him by rocking him and singing softly.

_____ 6. Rather than go to court, Mr. Hillman and the owner of the gas station agreed to have a lawyer ___ their disagreement.

_____ 7. Shakespeare's plays, a priceless ___ from the sixteenth and seventeenth centuries, have been enjoyed by generation after generation.

_____ 8. My cousin Bobby is the most ___ collector I know. He collects almost anything, from baseball cards to beer cans.

_____ 9. To show his ___ for her singing, the talent agent sent Mary flowers after she performed in a local theater.

_____ 10. Part of the charm of spring is that it's ___. It comes and goes so quickly that we can't wait for its return.

NOTE: Now check your answers to these items by turning to page 130. Going over the answers carefully will help you prepare for the next two practices, for which answers are not given.

Sentence Check 2

Using the answer lines provided, complete each item below with **two** words from the box. Use each word once.

_muted_____ 1–2. Loud music upsets our canary, but ___ tones ___ her.
_pacify_____

_____ 3–4. Leo is such a(n) ___ chef that his enthusiasm for cooking never ___s. He's been known to cook with great enthusiasm for ten straight hours.
_____

_____ 5–6. Becky's ___ for Gerald turned out to be ___. She discovered that he used drugs and could not condone° his habit, so she broke up with him.

_____ 7–8. In the Bible, King Solomon ___s a dispute between two women, each of
_____   whom contends° that a child is her own. To end the impasse°, the king
                                  suggests that the child be cut in two. This thought ___s horror in one of the
                                  women. The king then knows she is the real mother.

_____ 9–10. It is necessary to ___ a human infant because it is the biological ___ of
_____   newborn mammals to be unable to survive on their own. Parental care is
                                   indispensable°.

Final Check: *Getting Scared*

Here is a final opportunity for you to strengthen your knowledge of the ten words. First read the following
selection carefully. Then fill in each blank with a word from the box at the top of the previous page.
(Context clues will help you figure out which word goes in which blank.) Use each word once.

© Jacob Lund/shutterstock.com

   Do you remember trying to scare yourself and everybody
else when you were a kid? For instance, maybe you were
a(n) (1)_____ roller-coaster rider,
closing your eyes and screaming and loving every minute.
Afterward, you would (2)_____
your still nervous stomach by quietly sipping an ice-
cold Coke. If a short roller-coaster ride gave you too
(3)_____ a thrill, there was always the
long-term fear of a horror movie. If the horrors it depicted° were vile° enough, you might be scared about
going to bed for the next three months.

   And remember popping out from behind corners and yelling "Boo!" at your brother? The fight that
followed ("You didn't scare me one bit." "Did too." "Did not." "Did too.") would go on until a grown-
up (4)_____(e)d the conflict. (Parents always seemed to be there to settle
disputes among siblings or to (5)_____ and reassure you at times when you needed
support.)

   At other times, you and your friends probably sat around a campfire late at night, engaging in
your favorite nocturnal° activity—telling ghost stories. Thrilled with the horror of it all, you spoke in
voices so (6)_____ they were almost whispers. The storyteller who gained the most
(7)_____ was the one who could (8)_____ the greatest terror in
others. If anybody's fear started to (9)_____, this expert would build it up again with
the most effective story of all: the story of the ghost in the outhouse, a (10)_____
handed down from older brothers and sisters to younger ones. This traumatic° tale always made you so
scared that you needed to go to the outhouse. But fearing the ghost there, how could you?

Scores   Sentence Check 2 _____%   Final Check _____%

Enter your scores above and in the **Vocabulary Performance Chart** on the inside back cover of the book.

aloof	longevity
ambivalent	magnitude
augment	mundane
dispel	obscure
explicit	render

Ten Words in Context

In the space provided, write the letter of the meaning closest to that of each **boldfaced** word. Use the context of the sentences to help you figure out each word's meaning.

1 aloof
(ə-loof′)
-*adjective*

● Some people say that the British are **aloof**, but the British people I've met seem warm and open.

● I knew that Tyrell was upset with me about something because he was **aloof** even when I tried to be friendly.

___ *Aloof* means   A. motivated.   B. lazy.   C. cold.

2 ambivalent
(ăm-bĭv′ə-lənt)
-*adjective*

● "Because I'm **ambivalent** about marriage," Earl said, "I keep swinging back and forth between wanting to set the date and wanting to break off my engagement."

● I'm **ambivalent** about my counselor. I appreciate her desire to be helpful, but I dislike her efforts to interfere in my life.

___ *Ambivalent* means   A. meaning well.   B. having mixed feelings.   C. experienced.

3 augment
(ôg-měnt′)
-*verb*

● Why are women so willing to **augment** their height by wearing high heels when this kind of footwear is so bad for their feet?

● Because Jamila needed additional money, she **augmented** her salary by walking dogs before and after work.

___ *Augment* means   A. to add to.   B. to risk.   C. to cover up.

4 dispel
(dĭ-spěl′)
-*verb*

● Vickie's sweet note of apology was enough to **dispel** the slight anger Rex still felt toward her.

● I tried to **dispel** my friend's fears about her blind date that evening by telling her that my parents met on a blind date.

___ *Dispel* means   A. to cause.   B. to eliminate.   C. to communicate.

5 explicit
(ěks-plĭs′ĭt)
-*adjective*

● Even though the instructions were **explicit**, we were still unable to put the bookcase together.

● My parents were very **explicit** about what I could and could not do during their three-day absence. They presented me with a detailed list!

___ *Explicit* means   A. brief.   B. mysterious.   C. specific.

6 longevity
(lŏn-jěv′ĭ-tē)
-*noun*

● Toyotas and Hondas are known for their **longevity**, often outlasting more expensive cars.

● The animal with the greatest **longevity** is the giant land tortoise, which can live several hundred years.

___ *Longevity* means   A. form.   B. long life.   C. size.

7 magnitude
(măg′nĭ-tōōd′)
-noun

- Numbers in the billions and trillions are of too great a **magnitude** for most people to grasp.
- When the bank teller realized the **magnitude** of his error, he panicked at the thought of being held responsible for the loss of so large a sum of money.

___ *Magnitude* means   A. a great amount.   B. a time.   C. a length.

8 mundane
(mŭn-dān′)
-adjective

- Because Usha teaches belly dancing every day, it is simply one more **mundane** activity to her.
- The most **mundane** activities can turn into extraordinary events. For instance, I met my best friend while washing my clothes at the laundromat.

___ *Mundane* means   A. exciting.   B. painful.   C. commonplace.

9 obscure
(ŏb-skyōōr′)
-adjective

- The walls of the ancient tomb were marked with **obscure** symbols that no one could understand.
- The police easily recovered the stolen painting, but the identity of the thief remains **obscure**.

___ *Obscure* means   A. unimportant.   B. unclear.   C. known.

10 render
(rĕn′dər)
-verb

- Don't let the baby near your term paper with that crayon, or she will **render** it unreadable.
- Phyllis added so much red pepper to the chili that she **rendered** it too hot for anyone to eat.

___ *Render* means   A. to remember.   B. to make.   C. to wish.

Matching Words with Definitions

Following are definitions of the ten words. Clearly write or print each word next to its definition. The sentences above and on the previous page will help you decide on the meaning of each word.

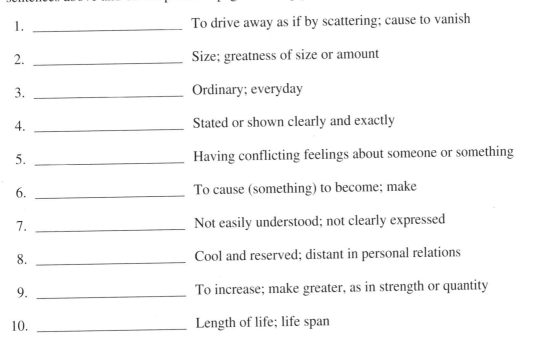

1. _____ To drive away as if by scattering; cause to vanish

2. _____ Size; greatness of size or amount

3. _____ Ordinary; everyday

4. _____ Stated or shown clearly and exactly

5. _____ Having conflicting feelings about someone or something

6. _____ To cause (something) to become; make

7. _____ Not easily understood; not clearly expressed

8. _____ Cool and reserved; distant in personal relations

9. _____ To increase; make greater, as in strength or quantity

10. _____ Length of life; life span

CAUTION: Do not go any further until you are sure the above answers are correct. Then you can use the definitions to help you in the following practices. Your goal is eventually to know the words well enough so that you don't need to check the definitions at all.

Sentence Check 1

Using the answer line provided, complete each item below with the correct word from the box. Use each word once.

A. aloof	B. ambivalent	C. augment	D. dispel	E. explicit
F. longevity	G. magnitude	H. mundane	I. obscure	J. render

_____ 1. When I'm frightened, I try to appear ___ because looking cool and distant helps me feel in control.

_____ 2. Recent research suggests that our parents' ___ doesn't necessarily affect how long we will live.

_____ 3. "Russell seems ___ toward me," Janice said, "as if he both likes and dislikes me."

_____ 4. The architect decided to add another pillar to the building to ___ its support.

_____ 5. The best writers can describe something ___ so that it doesn't seem ordinary at all.

_____ 6. I began to realize the ___ of the insect population when I read that there are more kinds of insects living today than all other kinds of animals in the world.

_____ 7. "I try to make my test questions as ___ as possible," said Mr. Baines, "so that my students will know exactly what answers I'm looking for."

_____ 8. If Claude proposes marriage to Jean, he will ___ any doubts she may still have as to whether or not he really loves her.

_____ 9. "If you keep walking on the backs of your shoes like that, you will ___ them as flat as the floor," Anya's mother said.

_____ 10. The essence of my science teacher's genius is that he is able to make complicated, ___ ideas clear to students.

NOTE: Now check your answers to these items by turning to page 130. Going over the answers carefully will help you prepare for the next two practices, for which answers are not given.

Sentence Check 2

Using the answer lines provided, complete each item below with **two** words from the box. Use each word once.

_____
_____ 1–2. I'm ___ about playing with our rock band. The music is a source of elation° for me, but I'm afraid it will ___ me deaf one of these days.

_____
_____ 3–4. Harriet was able to ___ the family income by working overtime. Although her fiscal° worries dwindled,° her problems with her husband and children increased in ___ as a result.

_____
_____ 5–6. When asked about his ___, ninety-year-old Mr. Greene gives a(n) ___ recipe for a long life: eat well, exercise, and stay away from hospitals. "It's ironic°," he explains, "that I got the worst infection of my life at a hospital."

_____   7–8. "Does the idea that we don't always see things as they really are seem ___
_____   to you?" the teacher asked. "If so, it will become clearer if you relate it to
                         the ___ experience of looking down a road. Doesn't it look narrower in the
                         distance than it really is?"

_____   9–10. Gail sometimes appears cold and conceited, but she is ___ only toward
_____   people whom she strongly dislikes. With all others, her usual genial° and
                          modest manner soon ___s any impression that she is snobby.

Final Check: *My Sister's Date*

Here is a final opportunity for you to strengthen your knowledge of the ten words. First read the following selection carefully. Then fill in each blank with a word from the box at the top of the previous page. (Context clues will help you figure out which word goes in which blank.) Use each word once.

© Kirill Savostikov/shutterstock.com

    I remember watching my older sister, Ruth, as she removed the last roller from her hair. We gaped° at the result. She somehow had (1)_____(e)d her hair limp as spaghetti. When Ruth started to cry, I tried to pacify° her with my usual gentleness: "Why are you such a crybaby about some stupid guy?"

    The guy was Steven Meyer. He and Ruth were going to a high-school dance. She'd had a crush on him for years, for reasons that were (2)_____ to me. (I had never been able to discern° what she saw in him.)

    When Ruth began to (3)_____ her makeup by applying some more powder, she gave a terrifying scream that probably reduced my (4)_____ by at least a year. She informed me between sobs that a pimple had just appeared on her nose, making her "look like a vile° witch." I studied her face, expecting a pimple of truly amazing (5)_____. Instead, I spotted a tiny speck. I tried to (6)_____ Ruth's worries: "So, it makes you look like a witch. Don't you want to look bewitching?" But she just began to cry again. I took this opportunity to go downstairs and wait for Steven Meyer.

    He arrived a half hour before Ruth was ready. In the meantime, while waiting for Ruth, we talked, and I tried to figure out exactly what Ruth saw in him. Finally, she appeared. Trying to look (7)_____, she came downstairs very slowly, wearing a cool, distant expression.

    When Ruth returned home later that night, her comment about the evening was both curt and (8)_____: "Totally rotten." She contended° that Steven, far from being extraordinary, had turned out to be deficient° in personality—"the most (9)_____ sort of person in the world." It seemed Ruth had bypassed feeling (10)_____ about Steven and gone straight from love to hate.

    It's just as well, since I've been married to Steven for ten years now.

Scores	Sentence Check 2 _____%	Final Check _____%

The box at the right lists twenty-five words from Unit Four. Using the clues at the bottom of the page, fill in these words to complete the puzzle that follows.

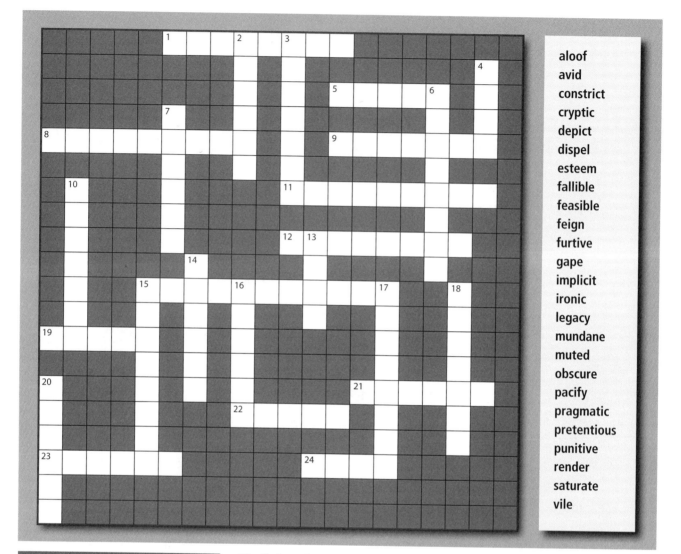

aloof
avid
constrict
cryptic
depict
dispel
esteem
fallible
feasible
feign
furtive
gape
implicit
ironic
legacy
mundane
muted
obscure
pacify
pragmatic
pretentious
punitive
render
saturate
vile

ACROSS

1. Suggested but not directly expressed
5. Cool and reserved; distant in personal relations
8. Practical
9. Ordinary; everyday
11. To make smaller or narrower, as by squeezing or shrinking
12. Capable of making an error
15. Making a show of excellence or importance, especially when undeserved
19. To pretend; give a false show of
21. Opposite to what might be expected
22. Softened; toned down, made less intense
23. To drive away as if by scattering; cause to vanish
24. Offensive to the senses, feelings, or thoughts; disgusting

DOWN

2. Something handed down from people who have come before
3. Having a vague or hidden meaning; puzzling
4. To stare in wonder or amazement, often with one's mouth wide open
6. Possible; able to be done
7. To make calm or peaceful
10. Not easily understood; not clearly expressed
13. Enthusiastic and devoted
14. To represent in pictures or words; describe
15. Giving or involving punishment; punishing
16. High regard; respect; favorable opinion
17. To soak or fill as much as possible
18. Done or behaving so as not to be noticed; secret; sneaky
20. To cause (something) to become; make

PART A

Choose the word that best completes each item and write it in the space provided.

_____ 1. While driving home three hours after her curfew, Lucille ___ an excuse she hoped her parents would believe.

    A. formulated   B. dispelled   C. ruptured   D. augmented

_____ 2. After a(n) ___ search during which I crawled around my entire apartment, my "missing" contact lens fell out of my eye.

    A. exhaustive   B. fiscal   C. pretentious   D. vindictive

_____ 3. After our car ran over a sharp rock, a tire ___. Luckily, we had a spare in the trunk.

    A. dispelled   B. gaped   C. ruptured   D. muted

_____ 4. It's ___ that my rich uncle is so stingy and my parents, who aren't rich, are always lending money to family members.

    A. exhaustive   B. ironic   C. furtive   D. pragmatic

_____ 5. Although he had heard about his grandmother's aches and pains a million times, Dennis ___ interest whenever she complained to him.

    A. condoned   B. feigned   C. mediated   D. reconciled

_____ 6. It's ___ of my uncle to call his family's second home his "estate in the country."

    A. punitive   B. transient   C. pretentious   D. muted

_____ 7. Peter hasn't been ___ about quitting his job, but he's hinted at it.

    A. explicit   B. avid   C. fallible   D. punitive

_____ 8. The preschooler's drawing ___ her parents, two brothers, and the "secret twin sister" she claims lives under her bed.

    A. depicted   B. condoned   C. mediated   D. nurtured

_____ 9. When my brother complained of a shortage of cash, his ___ message was "Can you lend me some money?"

    A. mundane   B. avid   C. implicit   D. detrimental

_____ 10. The poker gang laughed when Mom asked to join their game, but their ___ for her rose as she won the first four hands.

    A. esteem   B. longevity   C. legacy   D. magnitude

(Continues on next page)

PART B

On the answer line, write the letter of the choice that best completes each item.

_____ 11. When her toddler began shrieking in the middle of the crowded supermarket, the mother **pacified** the child by
A. shaking him and shouting, "Shut up!"
B. talking soothingly to him and offering him a pretzel.
C. continuing to push her shopping cart as though nothing were wrong.
D. glaring at the other customers as though the problem was their fault.

_____ 12. Roger realized Anitra's interest in him had **dwindled** when she began to
A. ask his friends if he was dating anyone special.
B. object to his seeing other women.
C. come up with excuses to call him at home.
D. avoid his phone calls and visits.

_____ 13. When my father **mediates** a quarrel, he
A. intentionally angers the people involved because he wants them to fight.
B. helps settle the quarrel by acting as a go-between.
C. takes one person's side in order to make the other one even angrier.
D. refuses to become involved in the quarrel in any way.

_____ 14. Although Vanessa developed a crush on her classmate Josh, the feeling was **transient** because
A. she asked him out on a date.
B. Josh was in all her classes.
C. she soon declared a different boy her "true love."
D. Josh returned Vanessa's feelings.

_____ 15. "I'm not **fallible**," my older sister insists. She means that she never makes
A. money.   C. mistakes.
B. meals.   D. good grades.

_____ 16. The **habitat** of a cactus is
A. very prickly.   C. grayish-green.
B. capable of storing water.   D. the desert.

_____ 17. A **mundane** experience, in most people's opinion, would be
A. grocery shopping.   C. sky-diving.
B. meeting one's future spouse.   D. having major surgery.

_____ 18. When Maria discovered that her son had lied to her, her **punitive** response was to
A. pretend she didn't know about the lie.   C. talk gently to him about lying.
B. spank him.   D. assume it was her fault.

_____ 19. "That chicken salad is **vile**," Cynthia said. "I
A. took one bite and gagged."   C. wish it were less spicy, though."
B. plan to ask our hostess for the recipe."   D. think it needs more curry powder."

_____ 20. A person who begins honking and yelling, "Go, go!" at other drivers the second a traffic light turns green is **deficient** in
A. vision.   C. patience.
B. rudeness.   D. speed.

Score	(Number correct) _____ x 5 = _____%

Enter your score above and in the **Vocabulary Performance Chart** on the inside back cover of the book.

PART A

Complete each item with a word from the box. Use each word once.

A. aloof	B. ambivalent	C. condone	D. contemplate	E. evoke
F. feasible	G. fiscal	H. inhibition	I. legacy	J. magnitude
K. muted	L. reconcile	M. render		

_____ 1. It isn't ___ to grow roses in our back yard. There's too much shade back there for roses.

_____ 2. Rosa has ___(e)d her son's temper tantrums for so long that he thinks they're acceptable behavior.

_____ 3. My love of the outdoors is a(n) ___ from my grandfather, who often hiked in the mountains.

_____ 4. The company is in such bad ___ shape that more than half the employees will soon lose their jobs.

_____ 5. At first, Tiffany was reluctant to sit in Santa Claus's lap, but she overcame her ___s when she saw that he was handing out candy canes.

_____ 6. As the wedding drew near, Brenda had to ___ herself to the fact that her son would marry a woman she disliked.

_____ 7. To make the bright green a more ___ shade, the painter added a few drops of black.

_____ 8. Music in a minor key often ___s sad feelings in the listener.

_____ 9. Satellite images revealed the ___ of damage from the floods, extending for hundreds of miles.

_____ 10. Cooking vegetables for too long ___s them less nutritious.

_____ 11. Tamika may seem ___, but she's not cold once she gets to know you.

_____ 12. Ivan has ___ feelings about his job. He loves the work but hates his boss.

_____ 13. Why ___ dropping out of school when you've got only two semesters to go?

(Continues on next page)

PART B

Write **C** if the italicized word is used **correctly**. Write **I** if the word is used **incorrectly**.

_____ 14. Eating sticky dried fruits can be as *detrimental* to your teeth as eating candy.

_____ 15. I asked Sal to *augment* the stereo because it was giving me a headache.

_____ 16. The suspect had a *furtive* expression; he must have been hiding something.

_____ 17. My grandfather's *pathetic* gardening won him two first prizes in the state flower show.

_____ 18. The poem is *obscure* because it jumps from one complicated image to another.

_____ 19. As Dad left for work, he called out his usual *cryptic* comment: "See you later."

_____ 20. *Saturate* the washcloth by wringing it out.

_____ 21. Female elephants join together to help each other *nurture* their young.

_____ 22. An *avid* reader, Judy spends much of her time enjoying newspapers, magazines, and books.

_____ 23. Being a *pragmatic* person, my brother values music and poetry more than practical things.

_____ 24. Some spiders have surprising *longevity*, living as long as twenty years.

_____ 25. Barry didn't let his children stay up late last night because he didn't want to set a *precedent* for future nights.

Score   (Number correct) _____ x 4 = _____%

PART A: Synonyms

In the space provided, write the letter of the choice that is most nearly the **same** in meaning as the **boldfaced** word.

_____ 1. **formulate**   A. recognize   B. aim for   C. develop   D. promote

_____ 2. **rupture**   A. accept   B. draw forth   C. burst   D. fill as much as possible

_____ 3. **implicit**   A. suggested   B. in conflict   C. devoted   D. brief

_____ 4. **precedent**   A. effect   B. earlier example   C. goal   D. main cause

_____ 5. **dispel**   A. recognize   B. oppose   C. drive away   D. create

_____ 6. **inhibition**   A. something handed down   B. holding back   C. tone   D. wish

_____ 7. **magnitude**   A. favorable opinion   B. length of life   C. location   D. importance

_____ 8. **render**   A. scatter   B. cause to become   C. increase   D. make narrower

_____ 9. **fiscal**   A. generous   B. physical   C. economic   D. expensive

_____ 10. **depict**   A. select   B. describe   C. ignore   D. expect

_____ 11. **pretentious**   A. acting important   B. fictional   C. practical   D. well-off

_____ 12. **evoke**   A. increase   B. make narrow   C. reply   D. bring forth

_____ 13. **mundane**   A. unlikely   B. ridiculous   C. commonplace   D. harmful

_____ 14. **saturate**   A. burst   B. make   C. soak   D. scatter

_____ 15. **gape**   A. look for   B. notice   C. see   D. stare

_____ 16. **condone**   A. forbid   B. put up with   C. encourage   D. imitate

_____ 17. **vindictive**   A. practical   B. complete   C. vengeful   D. surprising

_____ 18. **contemplate**   A. think about   B. decide   C. prefer   D. wait

_____ 19. **ambivalent**   A. active   B. sure   C. not harmful   D. having mixed feelings

_____ 20. **esteem**   A. curiosity   B. disapproval   C. acceptance   D. respect

_____ 21. **legacy**   A. promise   B. example   C. inheritance   D. increase

_____ 22. **feign**   A. pretend   B. conceal   C. develop   D. oppose

_____ 23. **habitat**   A. hobby   B. environment   C. lifestyle   D. diet

_____ 24. **longevity**   A. youth   B. good health   C. life span   D. death

_____ 25. **pacify**   A. care for   B. encourage   C. admire   D. calm down

(Continues on next page)

PART B: Antonyms

In the space provided, write the letter of the choice that is most nearly the **opposite** in meaning to the **boldfaced** word.

_____ 26. **dwindle**   A. replace   B. increase   C. reveal   D. improve

_____ 27. **exhaustive**   A. poorly stated   B. boring   C. impractical   D. incomplete

_____ 28. **reconcile**   A. contrast   B. accept   C. cause to vanish   D. decide to reject

_____ 29. **nurture**   A. dislike   B. win   C. neglect   D. fail to notice

_____ 30. **fallible**   A. perfect   B. beautiful   C. understandable   D. willing

_____ 31. **explicit**   A. poorly supported   B. lengthy   C. vague   D. complicated

_____ 32. **ironic**   A. strong   B. expected   C. true   D. covering few details

_____ 33. **vile**   A. organized   B. permanent   C. large   D. pleasant

_____ 34. **feasible**   A. manageable   B. impossible   C. surprising   D. delayed

_____ 35. **cryptic**   A. suggested   B. everyday   C. kind   D. clear

_____ 36. **genial**   A. not typical   B. impractical   C. unfriendly   D. foolish

_____ 37. **mediate**   A. prevent agreement   B. recognize   C. forget   D. be active

_____ 38. **obscure**   A. brief   B. disorganized   C. easily understood   D. correct

_____ 39. **pragmatic**   A. mistaken   B. impractical   C. offensive   D. untalented

_____ 40. **aloof**   A. friendly   B. mean   C. handsome   D. ambitious

_____ 41. **constrict**   A. admire   B. build   C. accept   D. make wider

_____ 42. **pathetic**   A. admirable   B. possible   C. broad   D. safe

_____ 43. **avid**   A. quiet   B. rare   C. unenthusiastic   D. impractical

_____ 44. **detrimental**   A. pleasant   B. helpful   C. respectful   D. clear

_____ 45. **augment**   A. decrease   B. oppose   C. deny   D. avoid

_____ 46. **furtive**   A. wise   B. successful   C. unhidden   D. impossible

_____ 47. **muted**   A. brightened   B. corrected   C. forbidden   D. out in the open

_____ 48. **deficient**   A. kind   B. having enough   C. useful   D. permanent

_____ 49. **punitive**   A. in favor of   B. organized   C. straightforward   D. rewarding

_____ 50. **transient**   A. frequent   B. permanent   C. rare   D. possible

Score   (Number correct) _____ x 2 = _____%

Each item below starts with a pair of words in CAPITAL LETTERS. For each item, figure out the relationship between these two words. Then decide which of the choices (A, B, C, or D) expresses a similar relationship. Write the letter of your choice on the answer line.

_____ 1. GAPE : AMAZING ::
    A. smile : sad
    B. laugh : humorous
    C. yawn : exciting
    D. interrupt : conversation

_____ 2. PUNITIVE : PENALTY ::
    A. liberating : shackles
    B. punishing : reward
    C. instructive : lesson
    D. verdict : evidence

_____ 3. CRYPTIC : CODE ::
    A. spicy : carrot
    B. encouraging : cheerleader
    C. wealthy : beggar
    D. mystical : magical

_____ 4. DETRIMENTAL : SMOKING ::
    A. beneficial : exercise
    B. physician : health
    C. snakebite : antidote
    D. harmful : medicine

_____ 5. RUPTURE : PIPE ::
    A. sweep : dustcloth
    B. dirt : shovel
    C. inhale : exhale
    D. malfunction : computer

_____ 6. VINDICTIVE : FORGIVING ::
    A. neglectful : attentive
    B. local : nearby
    C. expensive : costly
    D. take : revenge

_____ 7. CONTEMPLATE : IDEA ::
    A. study : textbook
    B. dinner : cook
    C. instructor : class
    D. ride : dog

_____ 8. HABITAT : ANIMAL ::
    A. house : garden
    B. house : apartment
    C. garden : plant
    D. plant : green

_____ 9. MEDIATE : CONFLICT ::
    A. begin : end
    B. enter : contest
    C. walk : run
    D. pay back : loan

_____ 10. FURTIVE : SPY ::
    A. tall : mouse
    B. sly : sneaky
    C. dishonest : criminal
    D. tiptoe : walk

(Continues on next page)

_____ 11. PACIFY : ENRAGED ::
  A. calm : asleep   C. preach : sermon
  B. heal : wounded   D. delay : tardy

_____ 12. DISPEL : FALSE RUMOR ::
  A. expose : conceal   C. sneeze : cold
  B. seal : crack   D. enclose : container

_____ 13. EXPLICIT : OBSCURE ::
  A. frequent : rare   C. expire : lapse
  B. usual : everyday   D. sow : seeds

_____ 14. MUNDANE : ORDINARY ::
  A. stone : diamond   C. sparkling : shiny
  B. bright : night   D. childish : adult

_____ 15. MAGNITUDE : MOUNTAIN ::
  A. agility : tortoise   C. magnify : microscope
  B. dampness : desert   D. sweetness : candy

_____ 16. CONSTRICT : SHRINK ::
  A. vanish : disappear   C. fracture : bone
  B. reverse : surprise   D. fire : ash

_____ 17. GENIAL : GRUMPY ::
  A. gentle : mild   C. selective : picky
  B. elegant : awkward   D. legible : readable

_____ 18. VILE : SPOILED FOOD ::
  A. rude : good manners C. shiny : new coin
  B. striped : long lines   D. medicine : bitter taste

_____ 19. ESTEEM : ROLE MODEL ::
  A. admiration : enemy   C. respect : fondness
  B. familiarity : stranger D. contempt : bully

_____ 20. MUTED : BLARING ::
  A. coarse : rough   C. functional : useless
  B. quiet : silence   D. external : outside

Score   (Number correct) _____ x 5 = _____%

Enter your score above and in the **Vocabulary Performance Chart** on the inside back cover of the book.

Appendixes

A. Limited Answer Key

IMPORTANT NOTE: Be sure to use this answer key as a learning tool only. You should not turn to this key until you have considered carefully the sentence in which a given word appears.

Used properly, the key will help you to learn words and to prepare for the activities and tests for which answers are not given. For ease of reference, the title of the "Final Check" passage in each chapter appears in parentheses.

Chapter 1 (Joseph Palmer)

Sentence Check 1
1. amoral
2. amiable
3. malign
4. encounter
5. adamant
6. eccentric
7. animosity
8. antagonist
9. absolve
10. epitome

Chapter 2 (Death of the Big Top)

Sentence Check 1
1. escalate
2. adjacent
3. acclaim
4. obsolete
5. tangible
6. elicit
7. terminate
8. methodical
9. exploit
10. engross

Chapter 3 (No Luck with Women)

Sentence Check 1
1. euphemism
2. assail
3. altruistic
4. allusion
5. mercenary
6. banal
7. arbitrary
8. syndrome
9. appease
10. taint

Chapter 4 (Accident and Recovery)

Sentence Check 1
1. conventional
2. comprehensive
3. flagrant
4. ponder
5. calamity
6. venture
7. fluctuate
8. turmoil
9. rehabilitate
10. persevere

Chapter 5 (Animal Senses)

Sentence Check 1
1. enigma
2. exemplify
3. dispatch
4. attest
5. enhance
6. attribute
7. mobile
8. orient
9. discern
10. nocturnal

Chapter 6 (Money Problems)

Sentence Check 1
1. nominal
2. prerequisite
3. constitute
4. concurrent
5. predominant
6. hypothetical
7. confiscate
8. default
9. recession
10. decipher

Chapter 7 (The New French Employee)

Sentence Check 1
1. implausible
2. intricate
3. vulnerable
4. sinister
5. suffice
6. intercede
7. degenerate
8. scrutiny
9. incoherent
10. sanctuary

Chapter 8 (A Cruel Teacher)

Sentence Check 1
1. contrive
2. blatant
3. gloat
4. blight
5. immaculate
6. plagiarism
7. qualm
8. gaunt
9. retaliate
10. garble

Chapter 9 (Learning to Study)

Sentence Check 1

1. incentive
2. indispensable
3. incorporate
4. devastate
5. Intermittent
6. succumb
7. digress
8. curtail
9. squander
10. rigor

Chapter 10 (The Mad Monk)

Sentence Check 1

1. infamous
2. cynic
3. virile
4. alleviate
5. intrinsic
6. demise
7. benefactor
8. speculate
9. revulsion
10. covert

Chapter 11 (Conflict Over Holidays)

Sentence Check 1

1. abstain
2. mandatory
3. diversion
4. benevolent
5. aspire
6. lucrative
7. agnostic
8. affiliate
9. dissent
10. deficit

Chapter 12 (Dr. Martin Luther King, Jr.)

Sentence Check 1

1. contend
2. prevalent
3. poignant
4. extrovert
5. Conversely
6. quest
7. traumatic
8. contemporary
9. charisma
10. proponent

Chapter 13 (Relating to Parents)

Sentence Check 1

1. rapport
2. prompt
3. flippant
4. congenial
5. prone
6. rationale
7. reprisal
8. perception
9. relentless
10. impasse

Chapter 14 (The Nightmare of Gym)

Sentence Check 1

1. nullified
2. elation
3. averse
4. ominous
5. detract
6. mortified
7. divulge
8. disdain
9. expulsion
10. endow

Chapter 15 (A Model Teacher)

Sentence Check 1

1. complacent
2. transcend
3. deplete
4. commemorate
5. waive
6. empathy
7. consensus
8. diligent
9. menial
10. niche

Chapter 16 (Shoplifter)

Sentence Check 1

1. condone
2. feasible
3. precedent
4. contemplate
5. gape
6. punitive
7. feign
8. pathetic
9. furtive
10. fiscal

Chapter 17 (Coffee Shop Blues)

Sentence Check 1

1. inhibition
2. detrimental
3. ironic
4. rupture
5. deficient
6. implicit
7. saturate
8. cryptic
9. vindictive
10. depict

Chapter 18 (Roughing It)

Sentence Check 1

1. formulate
2. constrict
3. reconcile
4. genial
5. vile
6. fallible
7. pragmatic
8. habitat
9. Pretentious
10. exhaustive

Chapter 19 (Getting Scared)

Sentence Check 1

1. nurture
2. muted
3. dwindle
4. evoke
5. pacify
6. mediate
7. legacy
8. avid
9. esteem
10. transient

Chapter 20 (My Sister's Date)

Sentence Check 1

1. aloof
2. longevity
3. ambivalent
4. augment
5. mundane
6. magnitude
7. explicit
8. dispel
9. render
10. obscure

B. Dictionary Use

It isn't always possible to figure out the meaning of a word from its context, and that's where a dictionary comes in. Following is some basic information to help you use a printed or online dictionary.

How to Find a Word

A printed dictionary contains many thousands of words. But if you know how to use guidewords, you can find a word rather quickly. *Guidewords* are the two words at the top of each dictionary page. The first guideword tells what the first word is on the page. The second guideword tells what the last word is on that page. The other words on a page fall alphabetically between the two guidewords. So when you look up a word, find the two guidewords that alphabetically surround the word you're looking for.

● Which of the following pairs of guidewords would be on the page with the word *skirmish*? (The answer to this and the questions that follow appear on the next page.)

skimp / skyscraper   **skyward / slave**   **sixty / skimming**

If you have access to the internet, you can visit a dictionary website and type the word you want to look up. And some computer programs, such as Microsoft Word, offer built-in dictionary tools.

How to Use a Dictionary Listing

driz•zle (drĭz′əl) *v.* **-zled, -zling.** To rain gently and steadily in fine drops.
— *n.* A very light rain. —**driz′zly,** *adj.*

A dictionary listing includes many pieces of information, as shown in the above example for *drizzle*. Note that it provides much more than just a definition. Key parts include:

Syllables. Dots separate dictionary entry words into syllables. Note that *drizzle* has one dot, which breaks the word into two syllables.

● To practice seeing the syllable breakdown in a dictionary entry, write the number of syllables in each word below.

glam•our _____   **mi•cro•wave** _____   **in•de•scrib•a•ble** _____

Pronunciation guide. The information within parentheses after the entry word shows how to pronounce the entry word. This pronunciation guide includes two types of symbols: pronunciation symbols and accent marks.

Pronunciation symbols represent the consonant and vowel sounds in a word. The consonant sounds are probably very familiar to you, but you may find it helpful to review some of the sounds of the vowels—*a, e, i, o,* and *u.* Every dictionary has a key explaining the sounds of its pronunciation symbols, including the long and short sounds of vowels. (See the Pronunciation Guide on the inside front cover of this book.)

Long vowels have the sound of their own names. For example, the *a* in *pay* and the *o* in *no* both have long vowel sounds. Long vowel sounds are shown by a straight line above the vowel.

In many dictionaries, the *short vowels* are shown by a curved line above the vowel. Thus the *i* in the first syllable of *drizzle* is a short *i*. The pronunciation chart on the inside front cover of this book indicates that the short *i* has the sound of *i* in *ill*. It also indicates that the short *a* has the sound of *a* in *apple*, that the short *e* has the sound of *e* in *end*, and so on.

● Which of the words below have a short vowel sound? Which has a long vowel sound?

drug _____   **night** _____   **sand** _____

Another pronunciation symbol is the *schwa* (ə), which looks like an upside-down *e* and has an "uh" sound. It stands for certain rapidly spoken, unaccented vowel sounds, such as the *a* in *above*, the *e* in *item*, the *i* in *easily*, the *o* in *gallop*, and the *u* in *circus*. Here are three words that include the schwa sound:

in•fant (ĭn′fənt)   **bum•ble** (bŭm′bəl)   **de•liv•er** (dĭ-lĭv′ər)

● Which syllable in *drizzle* contains the schwa sound, the first or the second? _____

Accent marks are small black marks that tell you which syllable to emphasize, or stress, as you say a word. An accent mark follows *driz* in the pronunciation guide for *drizzle,* which tells you to stress the first syllable of *drizzle.* Syllables with no accent mark are not stressed. Some syllables are in between, and they are marked with a lighter accent mark.

● Which syllable has the stronger accent in *sentimental*? _____

sen•ti•men•tal (sĕn′tə-mĕn′tl)

Parts of speech. After the pronunciation key and before each set of definitions, the entry word's parts of speech are given. The parts of speech are abbreviated as follows:

noun—*n.*   pronoun—*pron.*   adjective—*adj.*   adverb—*adv.*   verb—*v.*

● The listing for *drizzle* shows that it can be two parts of speech. Write them below:

_____   _____

Definitions. Words often have more than one meaning. When they do, each meaning is usually numbered in the dictionary. You can tell which definition of a word fits a given sentence by the meaning of the sentence. For example, the word *charge* has several definitions, including these two: **1.** To ask as a price. **2.** To accuse or blame.

● Show with a check (   ) which definition (1 or 2) applies in each sentence below:

The store charged me less for the blouse because it was missing a button.   1 ___   2 ___

My neighbor has been charged with shoplifting.   1 ___   2 ___

Other information. After the definitions in a listing, you may get information about the *origin* of a word. Such information about origins, also known as *etymology,* is usually given in brackets. And you may sometimes be given one or more synonyms or antonyms for the entry word. *Synonyms* are words that are similar in meaning to the entry word; *antonyms* are words that are opposite in meaning.

Which Dictionaries to Own

You will find it useful to own two recent dictionaries: a small paperback dictionary to carry to class and a hardbound dictionary, which contains more information than a small paperback version. Among the good dictionaries strongly recommended are both the paperback and the hardcover editions of the following: *The American Heritage Dictionary, The Random House College Dictionary,* and *Webster's New World Dictionary.*

Good online dictionaries include **www.ahdictionary.com** and **www.merriam-webster.com**.

Answers to the Dictionary Questions

Guidewords: *skimp/skyscraper*
Number of syllables: 2, 3, 5
Vowels: *drug, sand* (short); *night* (long)
Schwa: second syllable of *drizzle*

Accent: stronger accent on third syllable *(men)*
Parts of speech: noun and verb
Definitions: 1; 2

C. Topics for Discussion and Writing

NOTE: The first three items for each chapter are intended for discussion; the last three, for writing. Feel free, however, to either talk or write about any of the items.

Chapter 1 (Joseph Palmer)

1. Do you ever watch TV programs in which real-life antagonists appear and malign each other as the audience cheers and shouts? What do you think of these shows?

2. Think of some amiable people you know and also people who seem to feel a lot of animosity toward others. How do their relationships with others differ? Why might they deal with others as they do?

3. Do you think amoral people are born that way? Or is there another explanation for why some people have no conscience?

4. Write a paper on a point of view about which you are adamant. For example, you might feel strongly that children should be given a voice in certain family decisions. Or you might stubbornly insist that the government should offer free health care for all citizens regardless of age or income. In your paper, explain your reasoning.

5. Select a celebrity or someone you know who you think is the epitome of something—for example, the epitome of courage or talent or kindness. Write a paper in which you describe this person and give evidence for your opinion. You might begin with a sentence such as this: *My beloved Uncle John is the epitome of service to humankind.*

6. Who is the most eccentric person you have ever had an encounter with? Write a paper about two or three unusual things this person has done.

Chapter 2 (Death of the Big Top)

1. Do people who wear fur exploit animals, or are they making appropriate use of resources? Do you feel the same way about people who wear leather and eat meat?

2. Have you ever been in a conversation that was at first calm but then escalated into an angry argument? How did you (or the other person involved) eventually terminate the fight?

3. Name a book or movie that truly engrossed you and that you think is deserving of acclaim. What specifically about the book or movie elicits such admiration from you?

4. Pretend you're an advice columnist. One of your readers writes, "Dear _____, Occasionally, on the bus I take to work (or school), an attractive person sits in the seat adjacent to mine. How can I make contact?" Write a humorous, methodical plan for this reader to follow in order to meet the attractive stranger.

5. Have computerized calculators and spell-check programs made basic math and spelling instruction obsolete? Write a paper in which you defend one of these two points: (1) Schools should stop

spending so much time on math and spelling, or (2) Despite the common use of calculators and spell-check programs, schools should continue to emphasize math and spelling.

6. Select one of the following types of people: an athlete, a musician, an artist, a slob, a neat freak, a pack rat, or an animal lover. Write a paper in which you describe this imaginary person's apartment. What tangible evidence in the apartment would give hints of the owner's identity?

Chapter 3 (No Luck with Women)

1. Which is the most banal movie you've ever seen? Explain your choice by naming one or two ways in which the show lacks originality.

2. Are there rules and regulations at your school or workplace that seem arbitrary? Why do you think such seemingly unreasonable rules exist? Whom might they be intended to appease?

3. As you were growing up, what topics did people in your family consider unpleasant or offensive? Did family members tend to use euphemisms and make only vague allusions to these subjects? Or did they speak about them directly? Give an example to illustrate your point.

4. Who is the most mercenary of your friends or acquaintances? At the other end of the scale, which of your friends or acquaintances is the most altruistic? Write a paper that describes both people and indicates which one you prefer and why.

5. Do you sometimes feel assailed by homework, tests, and other school demands? Write a humorous paper about "Tired Student Syndrome," describing the symptoms of this imaginary "disease."

6. Has anyone ever spread a rumor about you that has tainted your reputation? If not, have you seen someone else's reputation damaged by rumors? Write about the rumor and its effects.

Chapter 4 (Accident and Recovery)

1. Pretend the superintendent of a prison for youthful criminals wants to rehabilitate the inmates and has consulted you. With your classmates, brainstorm ideas for such a program. The program can be as comprehensive as you like, involving any kind of treatment or education you think might help these young people turn their lives around.

2. Whom can you think of whose clothing and appearance are quite conventional? On the other hand, whom can you think of whose clothing and appearance show a flagrant disregard for what is considered normal? Describe in detail the two people's appearances, and suggest why they might have decided to look or dress as they do.

3. Think of someone you admire because of a risk he or she has taken. Perhaps the person gave up a steady but boring job to do something he or she really believed in, or maybe the person ventured failure by going back to school after being out of it for some time. What happened? In your opinion, is the person happy he or she took that risk?

4. Do you know anyone whose life seems to involve one calamity after another? Write a paper about this person, giving examples of events that have caused his or her life to be in turmoil. Do you think that the person has more than his or her share of bad luck? Or does he or she somehow contribute to the problems?

5. Think of a situation in your life in which you were tempted to give up, but instead kept trying. Perhaps you've struggled with a class, a sport, a personal relationship, or a job. In a paper, describe the situation and explain what made you persevere instead of giving up. Alternatively, write about such a situation in the life of someone you know.

6. Write about a difficult decision you've had to make. Describe how your thoughts fluctuated as you pondered what course of action to take. What did you finally decide to do, and why?

Chapter 5 (Animal Senses)

1. Which appeals to you more: living your life in one community where you'd "put down roots," or living a more mobile life, moving from place to place? Explain which way of life you'd prefer and why.

2. Think of a time when a friend has done something to enhance his or her appearance. Did you discern the change right away, or did it take some time? How did you react to the change?

3. Everyone seems to know at least one "Odd Couple," two people who seem so different that their attraction to one another is an enigma. Whom do you know, or know about, who exemplify such a mismatched couple? Why might they be together?

4. If you could design your own city or town, what attributes would it include? Write a paper listing and explaining some characteristics you feel would contribute to good lives for residents and make it easy for newcomers to orient themselves.

5. Choose a place you are familiar with both during the day and at night. Write a paper contrasting the place's daytime and nocturnal appearances. What sights, sounds, and other sensations might one experience at each time of day? You might describe, for instance, how a place that is unattractive in daylight becomes more attractive at night, when its ugliness is hidden. Or you might describe a place that is pleasant during the day but scary after dark.

6. Choose a character trait of one of your relatives. Then write a paper in which you attest to this trait's influence on your family life. For example, you might write about how your sister's bad temper has ruined some family activities or how your uncle's sense of humor has helped others get through some bad times. Add interest to your paper by using colorful descriptions and quotations.

Chapter 6 (Money Problems)

1. What, in your mind, constitutes lying? Does it occur only when a person says something he or she knows is not true? What about this hypothetical situation: Bill has a paper due the next day. The library is closed, and he doesn't have a printer at home. He says to his friend Ned, "I sure wish I knew someone who could let me use his printer." Ned says, "Good luck," and goes home. Then someone mentions to Bill that Ned has a printer at home. Later, Bill accuses Ned of lying, and Ned responds, "I never said I didn't have a printer. You never asked." Did Ned lie?

2. In your career as a student, what book have you been required to read that you found hardest to decipher? What was so difficult about it, and what (if anything) did you finally get out of it?

3. During a recession, soup kitchens, homeless shelters, and places that distribute donated clothing and food are very active. If you were in charge of such a place, would you provide services to the unemployed free of charge, or do you think it would be better to charge nominal fees? Explain your answer.

4. Imagine that you face two concurrent job offers: one paying $100,000 a year, and the other giving you the opportunity to travel for a year at someone else's expense. You can't accept both offers. There is no guarantee that either job will be available to you if you don't take it now. Write about the choice you would make and why you would make it.

5. What do you think are the predominant reasons so many people default on their car and house payments? Write a paper listing two or three of those reasons and explaining some ways to avoid failing to make such payments.

6. We often hear about situations in which authorities have confiscated large numbers of pets from abusive or neglectful households. These situations might be avoided if people were better prepared for the enormous responsibility of "parenting" numerous animals. Write a paper in which you explain two or three helpful prerequisites for people thinking about taking on several pets.

Chapter 7 (The New French Employee)

1. Which is easier to get away with—a simple lie or an intricate one? Give examples.

2. When you see the relationship between two friends or family members degenerate, what do you think is your best response? Should you intercede on behalf of the person you think is in the right, or should you keep your distance? Use situations from your experience to illustrate your points.

3. What are some implausible excuses you've heard (or perhaps given!) for not completing homework? Did any suffice to satisfy the teacher?

4. In school, people who are different in any way are often vulnerable to teasing, criticism, and even attack. Write a paper about a person you've known who was targeted for abuse because he or she was in some way different. Did anyone come to this person's defense?

5. When people adopt a dog from a shelter, they should be offering a sanctuary for an animal that doesn't have a home. Unfortunately, some dog adopters are not prepared to be pet owners. They may even have sinister motives for adopting animals. Pretend that you are in charge of checking out would-be dog adopters. Write a paper about the kind of scrutiny you would give before approving them. You might begin with a main idea such as this: *If I were in charge of checking out would-be dog adopters, I'd look for three things.*

6. Some people find it easy to speak up in public, while others tend to be incoherent when trying to speak in a group. Which are you? Write a paper about at least one experience that shows how easy or difficult speaking up in public is for you. If you like, use exaggeration to achieve a humorous tone.

Chapter 8 (A Cruel Teacher)

1. Why do you think plagiarism is considered such a bad thing in school and elsewhere? What is the most blatant case of plagiarism you've heard about?

2. After you have (or someone else has) retaliated against someone who has hurt or offended you, how do you usually feel? Do you gloat, bragging that you've gotten back at him or her? Or do you have some qualms about having sunk to that person's level? Give an example.

3. Text messages are easy to garble. Describe a time that a message you've left—or one you've received—was so jumbled that its meaning became confused.

4. How strongly are young people influenced by images on TV and in magazines? For instance, do very slender models and actresses encourage young girls to become unhealthily gaunt? Write a paper about a few ways young people imitate what they see in the media. Use detailed examples to support your points.

5. Where do you fall on the neatness scale? Are you a total slob? Does it drive you crazy if your room or house is anything less than immaculate? Write a humorous paper describing your housekeeping methods. Your main point might be stated something like this: *My housekeeping methods are weird but effective.*

6. What, in your opinion, is the single biggest blight on society today? Drugs? Guns? Pollution? Something else? Write a paper in which you explain your opinion as well as one or two solutions you've contrived for dealing with the problem.

Chapter 9 (Learning to Study)

1. Describe a time when you tried to curtail a bad habit, such as eating too much, texting too often, or biting your nails. Did it help to provide yourself with incentives, such as rewarding yourself with new jeans if you'd lose five pounds?

2. When you imagine losing all your belongings in a fire, you realize what is indispensable to you. If such a tragedy occurred and you could rescue only one object, what would it be? What are two other objects it would devastate you to lose?

3. Describe your perfect vacation. Where would it take place, and what activities would you incorporate into it?

4. "Youth is wasted on the young," one writer said, meaning young people (in the eyes of their elders, anyway) often squander their opportunities. What opportunity do you wish you had made better use of? What happened to keep you from taking full advantage of the situation—did you succumb to laziness, peer pressure, or something else? Write a paper about an opportunity you missed.

5. Write a paper that describes a mentally or physically exhausting experience you have had. Use sharp details to make the reader feel the rigor of the experience. Don't digress into other topics, such as why you were there or who else was with you. Simply write about the difficulty.

6. Who is the most effective teacher you have ever had? Write a paper that explains what made him or her so good. Also mention whether you always appreciated him or her, or whether your good opinion was intermittent—interrupted by periods when you thought the teacher was, for example, too tough or unfair.

Chapter 10 (The Mad Monk)

1. In your opinion, what really makes a male virile? Is it how he looks? How he treats other people? How he handles his responsibilities? What qualities are intrinsic to a manly male?

2. For most people, the idea of eating a potentially deadly meal would be met with revulsion. But in Japan, people pay large sums to dine on fugu, a kind of blowfish. Fugu is popular for its taste, but it is also infamous because parts of this fish are extremely toxic. Twenty-three people have died since 2000 after eating fugu. Chefs who know how to safely prepare it earn big salaries. Speculate on why people would risk their lives to eat a meal that carries the risk of death.

3. Have you had a favorite pet that died? What led to its demise? Explain what made the pet so special to you.

4. Cynics say that no one does anything simply to be kind. Write a paper that either agrees with or contradicts that view. If you hold the opposing view, offer the example of someone who has served as a benefactor to you, or to someone else, without expecting a reward.

5. What's the best way you know to alleviate the blues? Write a paper on a way (or ways) you cheer yourself up. Include a vivid example of each method you mention.

6. Children often carry on covert activities. For example, they may hide the fact that they use a flashlight to read under the blanket when they should be sleeping. Or they may try to keep adults from learning that they've skipped school. As a young child, what secret activities did you take part in? Write a paper describing one or more such activities. Tell what the experiences were like for you and what methods you used to keep from being caught. If you ever *were* caught, explain how you were caught and what the consequences were.

Chapter 11 (Conflict Over Holidays)

1. When you were younger, were there rules about mandatory behavior in your household that created dissent between you and your parents? What were they?

2. What career do you aspire to? Does that career attract you primarily because it is lucrative, or are there other reasons you are drawn to it?

3. Tell about your daily diet. Does it have a deficit of certain kinds of food? Too much of others? What do you consider a healthy diet for someone your age?

4. Who is the most benevolent person you know? Write a paper about that person and his or her acts of generosity, describing one or more such acts in detail.

5. What role does your tablet or smartphone play in your life? Is it an occasional diversion, a constant companion, or something in between? How much of a problem would it be for you to abstain from using it for a week? A month? Write a paper describing your device's role in your life and how you think you'd manage if you had to give it up.

6. Are you affiliated with any groups, such as extracurricular clubs, study groups, or volunteer organizations? Write a paper explaining the group's role in your life. What type of group is it? Why did you join? What activities are you involved in? Has your view of the group changed since you've joined it?

Chapter 12 (Dr. Martin Luther King, Jr.)

1. Which famous athletes and entertainers would you say have charisma? In your opinion, are the people who have that quality necessarily extroverts, or can a quiet person be magnetic and charming as well?

2. What do you think of NASA's quest for a way to put astronauts on Mars and maybe even to establish a human colony there? Are you a proponent of further space exploration, or do you think the government's money could be better spent in other ways?

3. Describe the most poignant book, movie, or television show that you've read or seen lately. Include details that show just what was so touching about it.

4. What traumatic event do you remember from your childhood? Conversely, what is one of your happiest childhood memories? Write a paper about either event, telling what happened and explaining what made the event so painful or happy for you.

5. Who is a contemporary figure that you greatly admire? Write a paper in which you explain which qualities in that person you particularly respect. Begin with a main idea similar to this: *I admire and respect _____ largely because of two of his/her special qualities.*

6. What do you contend are the two best reasons for going to college? Write a paper explaining and defending your point of view.

Chapter 13 (Relating to Parents)

1. Brothers and sisters, even those who are usually on congenial terms, sometimes tease and play tricks on one another. If you had a brother or sister (or a cousin or close friend) when you were younger, did you sometimes do things to annoy him or her? What was the reprisal, if any?

2. People's perceptions of behavior often differ. For instance, have you ever been accused of being flippant when you were in fact being serious? Do people sometimes think you're grouchy when you're not feeling that way at all? Explain. How do you convince people of your true intent or feelings?

3. With whom in your family do you have the best rapport? How is communicating with that person different from talking with other members of your family?

4. Write a paper about a time when you and another individual—perhaps a friend, a coworker, or a family member—had a disagreement and reached an impasse. What happened next? What was your rationale for how you acted?

5. Imagine that you have a friend who has very poor self-esteem. Perhaps he or she is relentless about putting himself or herself down. Write a paper about two or three techniques you might try in order to prompt your friend to feel better about him or herself.

6. When you are faced with a decision, are you prone to make it quickly—or to put it off as long as possible? Think about, for instance, how long it takes you to select which classes to sign up for, what gifts to buy, when to get a haircut, and whether to ask someone out on a date. Write a paper in which you give examples of your usual decision-making style.

Chapter 14 (The Nightmare of Gym)

1. Of all the movies you've ever seen, which would you say had the most ominous atmosphere? What made it so ominous?

2. If a troublesome student views school with disdain, does it do any good to threaten him with expulsion? What might be more effective ways of dealing with students' bad behavior?

3. Is it ever right to nullify the results of an election? Under what conditions?

4. We all have memories of special childhood occasions when we were filled with elation. Write a paper describing such an occasion in your childhood. Include any details and explanations needed for your reader to understand why the experience filled you with such joy or pride.

5. Although the details may be embarrassing to divulge, write a paper about an experience that really mortified you. Be sure to include specific information so that the reasons for your feelings will make sense.

6. Of the people you know, who is endowed with the best combination of physical, mental, and/or emotional qualities? Write a paper describing that person. Since no one is perfect, include one or two characteristics that detract from the person's otherwise outstanding personality and/or appearance. Your main idea for this paper might be similar to this: *Although Veronica does have her faults, she has a wonderful combination of personal qualities.*

Chapter 15 (A Model Teacher)

1. What are the two menial household tasks that you dislike the most? Is there a consensus on this question among your classmates?

2. When you imagine the lives of celebrities, surrounded by adoring fans and making incredible amounts of money, it's not hard to understand why these people develop attitude problems. Do you think you could deal with sudden wealth and fame without becoming complacent? How might you transcend the pressures of being a celebrity and remain a "regular person"?

3. Think about your future. What niche do you see yourself filling in ten years? What type of work do you think you'd like to be doing? What could you do now to learn about that activity to see if it's really what you imagine it to be?

4. Write a paper about two people in your life. One is a person for whom you have a lot of empathy because you think this person is trying hard to do a good job of managing his or her life. The other is a person who has depleted your store of sympathy, perhaps because he or she seems to be a complainer who does little to improve his or her situation. In your paper, contrast how the two people manage their lives and problems.

5. What do you wish you had been more diligent about when you were younger? Studying a particular subject? Practicing a musical instrument? Learning an athletic skill? Write a paper describing what you wish you'd worked harder at, and why.

6. Write a paper, humorous or serious in tone, in which you answer the following question: After your death many years from now, your friends and/or family want to commemorate your life in some fashion. What would be a suitable celebration held or memorial established in your honor? Your paper might take the form of instructions to your friends and family.

Chapter 16 (Shoplifter)

1. Everyone knows the tendency of drivers to slow down and gape at the scene of an accident. What do you think is the reason for this tendency? What drives people to stare at a horrible sight?

2. Do you condone using physical punishment, such as spanking, for children? Or do you think there are punitive techniques that work more effectively? What would these be? Explain.

3. When you were little, did you ever feign an illness in order to get out of doing something? Were you skillful enough to get away with it, or were your attempts to act sick pretty pathetic?

4. Write a paper comparing two routes your future might take. One route should be quite feasible—a practical, realistic plan. The other should be less realistic, even wildly unlikely, but lots of fun. Use humor to make your paper enjoyable to write and to read.

5. What's your fiscal style? Do you save for a future need? Spend money as soon as you have it? And how did you develop your style—are you following the precedent your family set for you? Write a paper about how you behave with money and why. You might state your main idea like this: *My money-management habits can be improved in a couple of ways.*

6. As you contemplate everything you've done in the current school year, which of your accomplishments are you proudest of? Why? Write a paper about your reasons for choosing this particular accomplishment.

Chapter 17 (Coffee Shop Blues)

1. You would think that when people grew up with situations that were detrimental to their well-being—for instance, with an abusive parent or with family members who are alcoholics—that they would be determined never to repeat that situation. It's an ironic fact, though, that people often do re-create those painful situations when they become adults. Why do you think people tend to repeat behaviors that they themselves have been hurt by? What might be done to help them change?

2. Do you know someone who seems to have an unusual number of inhibitions? Maybe the person refuses to do anything in public, such as dance or try a new activity, that might make him or her look silly. Are these people deficient in self-confidence, or could there be other reasons for their inhibitions?

3. How are chores divided up in your family? Has the family formally decided who should do what, or is there more of an implicit understanding about general areas of responsibility?

4. Write a paper in which you depict, hour by hour, a typical school day for you. Which parts of it do you enjoy the most? The least?

5. Have you, or has someone you know, ever been the victim of a vindictive act? Write a paper describing what the other person did and why—and what happened as a result.

6. Write about a time when a friend's cryptic behavior left you puzzled or disturbed. Perhaps someone with whom you'd been on good terms suddenly began acting unfriendly, or someone seemed busy with an activity he or she wouldn't talk about. Be sure to explain just what was puzzling about the behavior. If you eventually figured out what was going on, include that in your paper as well.

Chapter 18 (Roughing It)

1. When you hear about battles between housing developers and environmentalists concerned about protecting animals' habitats, whose side are you usually on? Which do you think is more important: to take care of people's housing needs, or to protect animals' homes? Explain your view.

2. A pretentious, know-it-all character appears in many TV comedies and movies. Think of such a character and describe how he or she makes a show of his or her importance.

3. Is there a situation in your life that you're not very pleased with, but you've had to reconcile yourself to? For example, maybe someone you care about is friendly with someone you don't care for. Or maybe a relative or teacher grouchy, but there doesn't seem to be much you can do about it. Explain what you've had to do to accept the situation.

4. We are probably all fallible in our first judgments of others. Write about a time when your initial judgment of another person was wrong. Perhaps you thought someone was unfriendly at first, but the person turned out to be quite genial when you got to know him or her better. Give specific examples of the person's behavior so that your reader can understand your reactions.

5. Think of a minor problem that's annoying you right now—such as a faucet that is leaking, a cat that is scratching the furniture, or your losing an assignment or a library book. In a paper, explain that problem. Then formulate a pragmatic solution to the problem, and explain that as well.

6. What do you know how to do very well? Paint a room perfectly? Make a delicious sandwich? Buy holiday gifts on a strict budget? Write exhaustive directions for doing something you're skilled in so a reader wishing to follow your instruction will benefit from your experience and have no trouble achieving good results.

Chapter 19 (Getting Scared)

1. Think of one legacy—a talent, an interest, a part of your physical appearance or way of behaving—that you've inherited from a relative. Tell about the relative and the legacy you've inherited. Are you glad or sorry that you have this trait in common?

2. What in your opinion are some of the most important things parents can do to nurture their children? Why might these things be so important to a growing child?

3. Have you ever been asked to mediate a disagreement between friends or family members? How did you respond? Were you successful in helping to pacify both people, or did one end up thinking he or she had been treated unfairly? Explain.

4. Write a paper about someone you once liked and respected, but who has lost your esteem. What happened to make your good opinion of this person dwindle?

5. Have you had the opportunity to revisit a place you knew well as a child—perhaps your or a relative's old home, your elementary school, or a place where you used to play? Write a paper about the experience of revisiting that place and the feelings and memories it evoked in you. Were those memories clear and strong, or dim and muted?

6. Write about an interest that you were avid about at one point in your life—a hobby or subject in which you were deeply involved. How did you become interested in it? Have you retained that interest, or was it transient?

Chapter 20 (My Sister's Date)

1. When have you faced a decision about which you were ambivalent? What made the decision so difficult? Did something finally happen to render the decision a little easier for you?

2. Do you enjoy reading material that is new and challenging, or do you prefer something more mundane? Give examples. Also, what are your techniques for dealing with reading assignments that are somewhat obscure?

3. Is there someone you've been friends with for many years? What do you think has contributed to the longevity of your friendship?

4. Write a description of someone who you think is aloof. Include explicit details about exactly what the person does that makes him or her seem so cool and distant.

5. Imagine that a friend who had dropped out of school was considering going back. But he or she is scared and says, "I don't know if I can succeed." Write a letter to your friend in which you do your best to dispel his or her fears. Include in your letter the point that education augments a person's chances for a successful career.

6. Write a paper about an important decision you've had to make recently. What about the decision made it a matter of great magnitude to you? How did you know it was the right decision?

D. Word List

Notes

Notes

Notes

Notes